EVOLVE

STUDENT'S BOOK

with Digital Pack

Leslie Anne Hendra, Mark Ibbotson,
and Kathryn O'Dell

5B

Shaftesbury Road, Cambridge CB2 8EA, United Kingdom

One Liberty Plaza, 20th Floor, New York, NY 10006, USA

477 Williamstown Road, Port Melbourne, VIC 3207, Australia

314–321, 3rd Floor, Plot 3, Splendor Forum, Jasola District Centre, New Delhi – 110025, India

103 Penang Road, #05–06/07, Visioncrest Commercial, Singapore 238467

Cambridge University Press & Assessment is a department of the University of Cambridge.

It furthers the University's mission by disseminating knowledge in the pursuit of
education, learning and research at the highest international levels of excellence.

www.cambridge.org
Information on this title: www.cambridge.org/9781009235532

First published with Digital Pack 2022

20 19 18 17 16 15 14 13 12 11 10 9 8 7 6 5 4

Printed in Poland by Opolgraf

A catalogue record for this publication is available from the British Library

ISBN 978-1-009-23085-8 Student's Book with eBook
ISBN 978-1-009-23551-8 Student's Book with Digital Pack
ISBN 978-1-009-23552-5 Student's Book with Digital Pack A
ISBN 978-1-009-23553-2 Student's Book with Digital Pack B
ISBN 978-1-108-40907-0 Workbook with Audio
ISBN 978-1-108-40881-3 Workbook with Audio A
ISBN 978-1-108-41195-0 Workbook with Audio B
ISBN 978-1-108-40519-5 Teacher's Edition with Test Generator
ISBN 978-1-108-41074-8 Presentation Plus
ISBN 978-1-108-41205-6 Class Audio CDs
ISBN 978-1-108-40800-4 Video Resource Book with DVD
ISBN 978-1-009-23185-5 Full Contact with Digital Pack

Additional resources for this publication at www.cambridge.org/evolve

ACKNOWLEDGMENTS

The *Evolve* publishers would like to thank the following individuals and institutions who have contributed their time and insights into the development of the course:

Asli Derin Anaç, **Istanbul Bilgi University**, Turkey; Claudia Piccoli Díaz, **Harmon Hall**, Mexico; Daniel Martin, **CELLEP,** Brazil; Daniel Nowatnick, USA; Devon Derksen, **Myongji University**, South Korea; Diego Ribeiro Santos, **Universidade Anhembri Morumbi**, São Paulo, Brazil; Esther Carolina Euceda Garcia, **UNITEC (Universidad Tecnologica Centroamericana)**, Honduras; Gloria González Meza, **Instituto Politecnico Nacional, ESCA (University)**, Mexico; Heidi Vande Voort Nam, **Chongshin University**, South Korea; Isabela Villas Boas, **Casa Thomas Jefferson**, Brasilia, Brazil; Ivanova Monteros, **Universidad Tecnológica Equinoccial**, Ecuador; Lenise Butler, **Laureate Languages**, Mexico; Luz Libia Rey G, **Centro Colombo Americano Bogotá**, Colombia; Maria Araceli Hernández Tovar, **Instituto Tecnológico Superior de San Luis Potosí**, Capital, Mexico; Monica Frenzel, **Universidad Andres Bello**, Chile; Ray Purdey, **ELS Educational Services**, USA; Roberta Freitas, **IBEU**, Rio de Janeiro, Brazil; Rosario Aste Rentería, **Instituto De Emprendedores USIL**, Peru; Verónica Nolivos Arellano, **Centro Ecuatoriano Norteamericano**, Quito, Equador.

To our speaking competition winners, who have contributed their ideas:

Alejandra Manriquez Chavez, Mexico; Bianca Kinoshita Arai Kurtz, Brazil; Gabriel Santos Hernández, Mexico; Gerardo Torres, Mexico; Giulia Gamba, Brazil; Hector Enrique Cruz Mejia, Honduras; Jorge, Honduras; Ruben, Honduras; Stephany Ramírez Ortiz, Mexico; Veronica, Ecuador.

To our expert speakers, who have contributed their time:

Bojan Andric, Carolina Hakopian, Jacqueline Castañeda Nuñez, Lucia D'Anna, Odil Odilov, Wendy Sanchez-Vaynshteyn.

And special thanks to Wayne Rimmer for writing the Pronunciation sections, and to Laura Patsko for her expert input.

Authors' Acknowledgments

The authors would like to extend their warmest thanks to the team at Cambridge University Press. They'd particularly like to thank Gillian Lowe and Nino Chelidze for their kind, thorough, and encouraging support.

Leslie Anne Hendra would like to thank Michael Stuart Clark, as always.

Mark Ibbotson would like to thank Nathalie, Aimy, and Tom.

Kathryn O'Dell would like to thank Kevin Hurdman for his support throughout the project and for his contribution to this level.

The authors and publishers acknowledge the following sources of copyright material and are grateful for the permissions granted. While every effort has been made, it has not always been possible to identify the sources of all the material used, or to trace all copyright holders. If any omissions are brought to our notice, we will be happy to include the appropriate acknowledgements on reprinting and in the next update to the digital edition, as applicable.

Key: REV = Review, U = Unit.

Text

U7: Interview text of 'Sofian and Nathalie'. Copyright © Nathalie Grandjean and Sofian Rahmani. Reproduced with kind permission of Mark Ibbotson; TalentSmart Inc. for the text from 'Why You Should Spend Your Money on Experiences, Not Things' by Travis Bradberry, Ph.D. Copyright © TalentSmart and Dr. Travis Bradberry. Reproduced with kind permission; **U8**: The Guardian for the adapted text from 'How to complain effectively' by Anna Tims, *The Guardian*, 18.02.2010. Copyright Guardian News & Media Ltd 2018. Reproduced with permission; **U9**: The Art of Manliness for the text from 'How to Make Small Talk with Strangers: My 21-Day Happiness Experiment' by John Corcoran, https://smartbusinessrevolution.com/. Copyright © Art of Manliness. Reproduced with kind permission; **U10**: Telegraph Media Group Limited and Michal Ben-Josef Hirsch for text 'Can you find your doppelganger in a day?' by Maxine Frith. Copyright © Telegraph Media Group Limited 2015 and Michal Ben-Josef Hirsch. Reprinted by permission of Telegraph Media Group Limited and Michal Ben-Josef Hirsch. All rights reserved; Monster Worldwide for the text from '8 ways to make your social media profile an employer magnet' by Mack Gelber. Copyright 2018 - Monster Worldwide, Inc. All Rights Reserved. **U11**: SiteSell Inc. for the text from 'Fake Reviews: Spot 'em and Stop 'em!' by Ken Envoy. Copyright © Ken Evoy, Founder & CEO of SiteSell. Reproduced with kind permission; **U12**: Interview text of 'Kevin Hurdman'. Copyright © Kathryn O'Dell with Kevin Hurdman. Reproduced with kind permission.

Photography

The following photographs are sourced from Getty Images.

U7–**U12**: Tom Merton/Caiaimage; **U7**: Barcroft Media; Flying Colours Ltd/DigitalVision; Ariel Skelley/Photodisc; Nancy Honey/Cultura; Sophie Powell/EyeEm; wanderluster/iStock/Getty Images Plus; kolderal/Moment; Bread and Butter/DigitalVision; Erik Isakson; Franz Pritz/Picture Press/Getty Images Plus; Elizabeth Beard/Moment; maurizio siani/Moment; maurizio siani/Moment; Barry Winiker/Stockbyte; **U8**: 10'000 Hours/DigitalVision; momentimages; Louis Turner; Alexander Walter/DigitalVision; Abraham/Moment; Mikael Dubois/Publisher Mix; Igor Golovniov/EyeEm; aluxum/iStock/Getty Images Plus; PhotoAlto/Frederic Cirou; 3alexd/iStock/Getty Images Plus; TokioMarineLife/iStock/Getty Images Plus; PhonlamaiPhoto/iStock/Getty Images Plus; RapidEye/E+; Suparat Malipoom/EyeEm; frema/iStock/Getty Images Plus; monkeybusinessimages/iStock/Getty Images Plus; U9: Boston Globe; Andrew Brookes/Cultura; 10'000 Hours/DigitalVision; Rubberball/Mike Kemp; Michael Blann/DigitalVision; Dan Dalton/Caiaimage; GoodLifeStudio/DigitalVision Vectors; Fentino/E+; The AGE/Fairfax Media; miodrag ignjatovic/E+; fstop123/E+; **REV3**: Sky Noir Photography by Bill Dickinson/Moment; **U10**: Trevor Williams/DigitalVision; Juanmonino/E+; Fuse/Corbis; Ken Reid/The Image Bank/Getty Images Plus; xavierarnau/E+; maxicake/iStock/Getty Images Plus; Junior Gonzalez; YinYang/E+; kupicoo/E+; Jose Luis Pelaez/Photodisc; Maskot; sturti/E+; twomeows/Moment; **U11**: VCG/Visual China Group; TANG CHHIN SOTHY/AFP; PHILIPPE LOPEZ/AFP; anilakkus/iStock/Getty Images Plus; Donald Bowers/Stringer/Getty Images Entertainment; NASA/Handout/Getty Images News; SeppFriedhuber/E+; JohnnyGreig/E+; Stephen Marks/The Image Bank/Getty Images Plus; cglade/iStock/Getty Images Plus; KatarzynaBialasiewicz/iStock/Getty Images Plus; Nataba/iStock/Getty Images Plus; AndreyPopov/iStock/Getty Images Plus; **U12**: ANDY BUCHANAN/AFP; Devon Strong/The Image Bank/Getty Images Plus; Roberto Ricciuti/GettyImages Entertainment; FabianCode/DigitalVision Vectors; mrPliskin/iStock/Getty Images Plus; sal73it/iStock/Getty Images Plus; Tetra Images; Carlos Alvarez/Stringer/Getty Images Entertainment; DenKuvaiev/iStock/Getty Images Plus; Nick Dolding/DigitalVision; Westend61; Indeed; Flashpop/DigitalVision; trinetuzun/iStock/Getty Images Plus; **REV4**: Stephan Zirwes; gawrav/E+.

The following photographs are source from other libraries/sources.

U10: Copyright © Telegraph Media Group Limited 2015; **U12**: Copyright © JD Dworkow.

Front cover photography by Bernhard Lang/Stone/Getty Images Plus/Getty Images.

Illustrations

U9: Ana Djordjevic (Astound US); **U12**: Lyn Dylan (Sylvie Poggio Artists Agency).

Audio production by CityVox, New York.

EVOLVE

SPEAKING MATTERS

EVOLVE is a six-level American English course for adults and young adults, taking students from beginner to advanced levels (CEFR A1 to C1).

Drawing on insights from language teaching experts and real students, EVOLVE is a general English course that gets students speaking with confidence.

This student-centered course covers all skills and focuses on the most effective and efficient ways to make progress in English.

Confidence in teaching.
Joy in learning.

Better Learning WITH EVOLVE

Better Learning is our simple approach where insights we've gained from research have helped shape content that drives results. Language evolves, and so does the way we learn. This course takes a flexible, student-centered approach to English language teaching.

Meet our expert speakers

Our expert speakers are highly proficient non-native speakers of English living and working in the New York City area.

Videos and ideas from our expert speakers feature throughout the Student's Book for you to respond and react to.

Scan the QR codes below to listen to their stories.

Wendy Sanchez-Vaynshteyn
from Bolivia
Data scientist

Bojan Andric
from Serbia
Interpreter

Carolina Hakopian
from Brazil
Dentist

Jacqueline Castañeda Nuñez
from Mexico
Urbanist

Lucia D'Anna
from Italy
Lead Promotion Specialist

Odil Odilov
from Tajikistan
Finance Assistant

INSIGHT

Research shows that achievable speaking role models can be a powerful motivator.

CONTENT

Bite-sized videos feature expert speakers talking about topics in the Student's Book.

RESULT

Students are motivated to speak and share their ideas.

Student-generated content

EVOLVE is the first course of its kind to feature real student-generated content. We spoke to over 2,000 students from all over the world about the topics they would like to discuss in English and in what situations they would like to be able to speak more confidently. Their ideas are included throughout the Student's Book.

"It's important to provide learners with interesting or stimulating topics."

Teacher, Mexico (Global Teacher Survey, 2017)

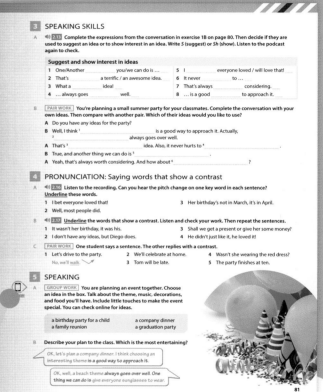

Find it

FIND IT

INSIGHT

Research with hundreds of teachers and students across the globe revealed a desire to expand the classroom and bring the real world in.

CONTENT

Find it are smartphone activities that allow students to bring live content into the class and personalize the learning experience with research and group activities.

RESULT

Students engage in the lesson because it is meaningful to them.

Designed for success

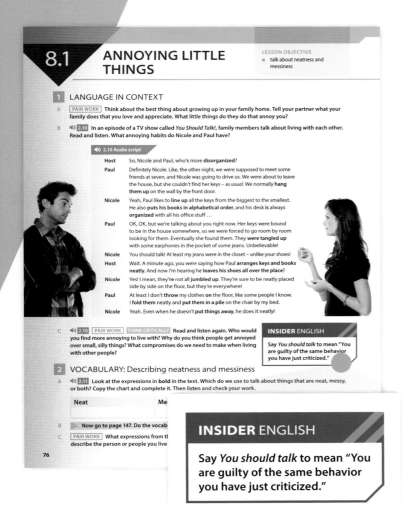

8.1 ANNOYING LITTLE THINGS

LESSON OBJECTIVE
■ talk about neatness and messiness

1 LANGUAGE IN CONTEXT

A PAIR WORK Think about the best thing about growing up in your family home. Tell your partner what your family does that you love and appreciate. What little things do they do that annoy you?

B 2.10 In an episode of a TV show called *You Should Talk!*, family members talk about living with each other. Read and listen. What annoying habits do Nicole and Paul have?

2.10 Audio script

Host	So, Nicole and Paul, who's more **disorganized**?
Paul	Definitely Nicole. Like, the other night, we were supposed to meet some friends at seven, and Nicole was going to drive us. We were about to leave the house, but she couldn't find her keys – as *usual*. We normally **hang them up** on the wall by the front door.
Nicole	Yeah, Paul likes to **line up** all the keys from the biggest to the smallest. He also **puts his books in alphabetical order**, and his desk is always **organized** with all his office stuff …
Paul	OK, OK, but we're talking about you right now. Her keys were bound to be in the house somewhere, so we were forced to go room by room looking for them. Eventually she found them. They **were tangled up** with some earphones in the pocket of some jeans. Unbelievable!
Nicole	You should talk! At least my jeans were in the closet – unlike your shoes!
Host	Wait. A minute ago, you were saying how Paul **arranges keys and books neatly**. And now I'm hearing he **leaves his shoes all over the place**?
Nicole	Yes! I mean, they're not all **jumbled up**. They're sure to be neatly placed side by side on the floor, but they're everywhere!
Paul	At least I don't **throw my clothes** on the floor, like some people I know. I **fold them** neatly and **put them in a pile** on the chair by my bed.
Nicole	Yeah. Even when he doesn't **put things away**, he does it neatly!

C 2.10 PAIR WORK THINK CRITICALLY Read and listen again. Who would you find more annoying to live with? Why do you think people get annoyed over small, silly things? What compromises do we need to make when living with other people?

INSIDER ENGLISH
Say *You should talk* to mean "You are guilty of the same behavior you have just criticized."

2 VOCABULARY: Describing neatness and messiness

A 2.11 Look at the expressions in bold in the text. Which do we use to talk about things that are neat, messy, or both? Copy the chart and complete it. Then listen and check your work.

Neat	Me...

B Now go to page 147. Do the vocab...

C PAIR WORK What expressions from th... describe the person or people you live...

76

INSIDER ENGLISH

Say *You should talk* to mean "You are guilty of the same behavior you have just criticized."

Pronunciation

INSIGHT

Research shows that only certain aspects of pronunciation actually affect comprehensibility and inhibit communication.

CONTENT

EVOLVE focuses on the aspects of pronunciation that most affect communication.

RESULT

Students understand more when listening and can be clearly understood when they speak.

Insider English

INSIGHT

Even in a short exchange, idiomatic language can inhibit understanding.

CONTENT

Insider English focuses on the informal language and colloquial expressions frequently found in everyday situations.

RESULT

Students are confident in the real world.

8.4 A SMILE GOES A LONG WAY

LESSON OBJECTIVE
■ write a complaint letter

1 READING

A Have you ever made a formal complaint? What was the problem? Was your complaint effective?

B IDENTIFY WRITER'S PURPOSE Read the article. What's its purpose? What specific examples of customer problems does the writer mention? Which are valid reasons for complaints?

Do you have a problem with a product, service, or company? It might be time to make a formal complaint. Anna Tims, a writer who focuses on consumer affairs, offers a list of tips for successful complaining. The secret is getting a lot of small things right.

HOW TO COMPLAIN EFFECTIVELY

Most large companies get hundreds of complaints – some silly and some serious. No matter how important your complaint is to you, it will just be added to a pile of complaints that a stressed-out customer service worker needs to read. So to be sure it makes the biggest impact, you must know how to state your complaint effectively. Follow these steps, and you're bound to get your problems solved.

☑ MAKE SURE YOUR COMPLAINT IS VALID
Your concern needs to be realistic. For example, if fees for ending a cell phone service contract early stop you from going to a cheaper cell phone service provider, that's too bad. You should have understood the contract. If, however, you have received poor service, you have the right to end your contract early. Or if you dropped your product and then stepped on it accidentally, it's your fault. But if a product breaks when you set it down gently, it's sure to be faulty.

☑ FIGURE OUT WHAT YOU WANT TO ACHIEVE
Do you want a refund, a replacement, or simply an apology? If you want a refund, you have to act quickly or you might lose your right to one. If you complain by phone, make a note of who you spoke to and when, and follow up the call with a letter restating your complaint and the response you got on the phone. Do the same if you sent the complaint through the company's website, so you have a record of it.

☑ ALWAYS ADDRESS A LETTER TO A SPECIFIC PERSON
It is best to start with the customer service manager. (If you aim too high – for example, the company president – you will be waiting while your letter is passed around until it reaches the right person.) Find out the manager's name and use their full title – Dr., Mr., Mrs., or Ms. A little thing like using someone's name can make a big impression.

☑ INCLUDE YOUR DETAILS
Remember to include your full name, address, and any order or reference numbers near the top of the letter. If a company can't easily find you in their system, they may not respond.

☑ KEEP COPIES
Make copies of all relevant documents – such as receipts, bank statements, order forms, and advertisements – and include them to support your complaint. If you want a new but stained couch replaced, include a photo of the damage.

☑ CHECK YOUR SPELLING
Carelessly written letters suggest you are as sloppy as the company you are complaining about.

☑ BE POLITE AND REASONABLE
Whether you are writing or calling, stay calm. Anger will give companies an excuse to refuse to deal with you.

☑ NAME NAMES
If you mention the unhelpful attitude of, for example, a store manager or customer service representative, try to include their names.

☑ SET A DEADLINE
Give the company a deadline for sending a useful response – 14 days is fair. Make a note of the date so you can increase the pressure if it is missed.

☑ MAKE SURE YOUR COMPLAINT ARRIVES
Send all letters by certified mail or special delivery so the company can't deny receiving them. If you use email, ask the person to confirm once they get it.

GLOSSARY
consumer affairs (n) a system related to protecting people who buy products and services
faulty (adj) not perfectly made or does not work correctly
sloppy (adj) not being careful or making an effort

Adapted from an article by Anna Tims in The Guardian

C Read the article again. Which points apply to (1) both a complaint letter and a phone call and (2) only a complaint letter?

D PAIR WORK THINK CRITICALLY Which three points in the article do you think would be the most effective? Why? Are there any points that won't have an effect? Why not?

82

2 WRITING

A Read Karen's letter to the customer service manager of Markus Appliances. What's the problem? Why is she not happy with the sales manager's response? What does she want?

> **To:** Mr. Edwards
> **From:** Karen Rebecca Mason
> **Subject:** RE: Faulty SUPERWASH Washing Machine, model number RGM205
>
> Reply Forward
>
> Dear Mr. Edwards,
> I am writing to complain about the above washing machine, which I bought during your Summer Sale on July 15. I purchased it for $175.99 at the Main Street branch of Markus Appliances and include a copy of the receipt as proof of purchase.
> After the machine was delivered, I tried to use it, but it wouldn't turn on. I checked the connection, which was fine, but the machine had no power. I immediately returned to the store and explained the problem to the sales manager, Rob Clark. At first, he suggested there was something wrong with the power in my house. When I insisted that the machine was faulty, he said, "Sorry, but you bought it during the half-price sale. We don't accept the return of sale items."
> I find this unacceptable. First, the item is obviously faulty. Second, your company advertisement (copy included) states that you accept all returns without question. I believe that includes sale items. Third, I feel Mr. Clark should be friendlier. It's a small thing, but a smile goes a long way.
> I would like your company to pick up the washing machine from my house and send me a refund of $175.99. I look forward to hearing from you within the next ten days.
> Sincerely,
> Karen Rebecca Mason

B PAIR WORK THINK CRITICALLY Which of the tips in the article in exercise 1A on page 82 did Karen follow?

C AVOID RUN-ON SENTENCES AND SENTENCE FRAGMENTS Read about two kinds of sentences to avoid in more formal writing. Look at the examples below. How could they be improved? Then find good versions of each in Karen's letter in exercise 2A.

Run-on sentences (They go on and on.)
1 I am writing to complain about the above washing machine, which I bought during your Summer Sale on July 15 for $175.99 at the Main Street branch of Markus Appliances and for which I include a copy of the receipt as proof of purchase.

Sentence fragments (Incomplete sentences)
2 Went back to the store. Explained problem to sales manager Rob Clark.
3 Unacceptable. First, obviously faulty.

✍ WRITE IT

D PLAN You're going to write a complaint letter. Choose an idea in the box or something you experienced yourself. With a partner, describe the problem and how you want the company to solve it. Then look at the letter in exercise 2A. What type of information should each paragraph contain in a complaint letter? How will you start and end the letter?

a bad restaurant meal	a broken or faulty item or package
poor customer service	an item that's different from the advertisement

E Write your complaint letter.

REGISTER CHECK

In formal written complaints, we often use expressions like *I find*, *I feel*, *I believe*, or *I think* to make statements less direct and more polite.

Direct
This is unacceptable.
Mr. Clark should be friendlier.

Less direct
I find this unacceptable.
I feel Mr. Clark should be friendlier.

83

Register check

REGISTER CHECK

In formal written complaints, we often use expressions like *I find, I feel, I believe,* or *I think* to make statements less direct and more polite.

Direct
This is unacceptable.
Mr. Clark should be friendlier.

Less direct
I find this unacceptable.
I feel Mr. Clark should be friendlier.

INSIGHT
Teachers report that their students often struggle to master the differences between written and spoken English.

CONTENT
Register check draws on research into the Cambridge English Corpus and highlights potential problem areas for learners.

RESULT
Students transition confidently between written and spoken English and recognize different levels of formality as well as when to use them appropriately.

> "The presentation is very clear, and there are plenty of opportunities for student practice and production."

Jason Williams, Teacher, Notre Dame Seishin University, Japan

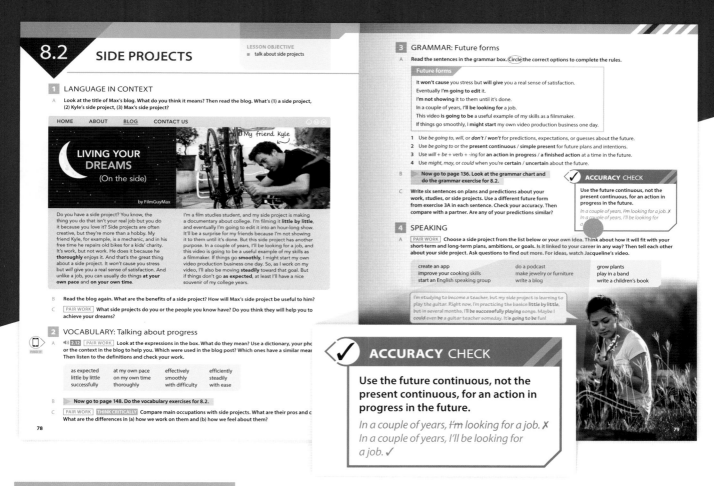

Accuracy check

INSIGHT

Some common errors can become fossilized if not addressed early on in the learning process.

CONTENT

Accuracy check highlights common learner errors (based on unique research into the Cambridge Learner Corpus) and can be used for self-editing.

RESULT

Students avoid common errors in their written and spoken English.

You spoke. We listened.

Students told us that speaking is the most important skill for them to master, while teachers told us that finding speaking activities which engage their students and work in the classroom can be challenging.

That's why EVOLVE has a whole lesson dedicated to speaking: Lesson 5, *Time to speak*.

Time to speak

INSIGHT

Speaking ability is how students most commonly measure their own progress, but is also the area where they feel most insecure. To be able to fully exploit speaking opportunities in the classroom, students need a safe speaking environment where they can feel confident, supported, and able to experiment with language.

CONTENT

Time to speak is a unique lesson dedicated to developing speaking skills and is based around immersive tasks which involve information sharing and decision making.

RESULT

Time to speak lessons create a buzz in the classroom where speaking can really thrive, evolve, and take off, resulting in more confident speakers of English.

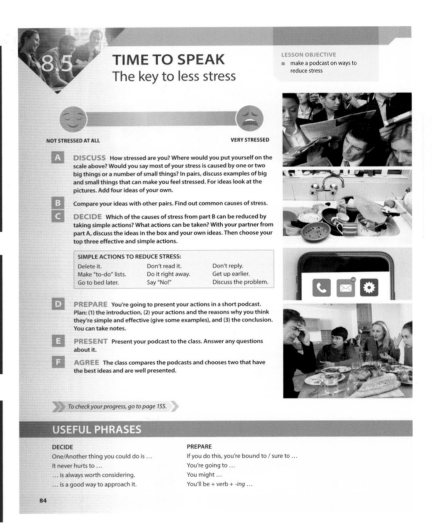

Experience Better Learning with EVOLVE: a course that helps both teachers and students on every step of the language learning journey.

Speaking matters. Find out more about creating safe speaking environments in the classroom.

EVOLVE unit structure

Unit opening page

Each unit opening page activates prior knowledge and vocabulary and immediately gets students speaking.

Lessons 1 and 2

These lessons present and practice the unit vocabulary and grammar in context, helping students discover language rules for themselves. Students then have the opportunity to use this language in well-scaffolded, personalized speaking tasks.

Lesson 3

This lesson is built around an off-the-page dialogue that practices listening skills. It also models and contextualizes useful speaking skills. The final speaking task draws on the language and strategies from the lesson.

Lesson 4

This is a skills lesson based around an engaging reading text. Each lesson asks students to think critically and ends with a practical writing task.

Lesson 5

Time to speak is an entire lesson dedicated to developing speaking skills. Students work on collaborative, immersive tasks which involve information sharing and decision making.

CONTENTS

This page is intentionally left blank

UNIT OBJECTIVES

- discuss worthwhile experiences
- talk about purchases
- bargain for a purchase
- write a for-and-against essay
- negotiate a boat trip

PRIORITIES

7

START SPEAKING

A   Where do you think these children are going? What are the risks? Is it worth it?

B   In your opinion, what kind of things are worth taking risks for? Why?

C   How do you define "worth"? Who, or what, do you value most in the world? Why? For ideas, watch Odil's video.

EXPERT SPEAKER

Are the types of things that Odil values, and his reasons for valuing them, similar to your ideas?

WORTHY HELPERS

1 LANGUAGE IN CONTEXT

A GROUP WORK THINK CRITICALLY What do you understand by the term "emergency services"? What type of jobs do they include? What qualities do people need to do these jobs? Why do you think they choose to do them?

B 🔊 2.02 Read and listen to Sofian and Nathalie talking about their jobs. What do they do? When did they choose their future careers? Does their work make them happy?

🔊 2.02 Audio script

Sofian It's common to dream about driving a fire truck when you're a kid. But I didn't think about being a firefighter until I was 14. I was in a traffic accident, and my foot was broken. It was a horrible situation to be in. But then the firefighters arrived, and suddenly I had people to help me and calm voices to **reassure me**. It was incredible having such an amazing team around me. At that moment, I decided I wanted to **devote my life to** that profession. And today, it's my job. Actually, it's more than just a job. I believe I'm doing something that **is worthwhile** – I'm **a good influence on** others, like those firefighters were on me. It**'s an honor** to be **making a contribution** like that. Plus, driving a fire truck is a seriously cool thing to do!

Nathalie For me, it's important to have contact with people and especially to be helpful. I don't just mean helping medically. I **take pleasure in** that side of the job, but I think I **get more satisfaction out of** the interpersonal side. It can be scary being in the hospital, and some patients have trouble coping. It**'s** really **beneficial** if they have someone to talk to. So for me, it's rewarding to spend time **reassuring patients**. When I decided as a teenager to become a nurse, I guess it was the medical side that interested me. But now I find it's the human side that I **value** the most. That's where I feel I can really **be of use** and **make a difference**.

C 🔊 2.02 Read and listen again. What aspects of their work do Sofian and Nathalie enjoy? What would and wouldn't you like about doing the two jobs?

FIND IT

2 VOCABULARY: Positive experiences

A 🔊 **2.03** Look at the expressions in the box. Can you guess their meaning from the way they are used in the texts in exercise 1B on page 66? Describe each one using other words. Use a dictionary or your phone to help you. Then listen and check your work.

be a good influence on	be an honor	be beneficial	be of use
be worthwhile	devote my life to	get satisfaction out of	make a contribution
make a difference	reassure sb	take pleasure in	value sth

B ▶ **Now go to page 147. Do the vocabulary exercises for 7.1.**

EXPERT SPEAKER

Was your experience similar to Odil's?

C **PAIR WORK** Have you ever been in a situation where you were helped by someone in a caring profession? Describe the situation. How did you feel? For ideas, watch Odil's video.

3 GRAMMAR: Gerunds and infinitives after adjectives, nouns, and pronouns

A Read the sentences in the grammar box. Complete the rules with words in the box.

> ### Gerunds and infinitives after adjectives, nouns, and pronouns
>
> It's **common to dream** about driving a fire truck.
>
> I had **people to help** me.
>
> They have **someone to talk to**.
>
> It can be **scary being** in the hospital.
>
> It's rewarding to **spend time reassuring** patients.

gerunds	infinitives	gerunds or infinitives

1 You can use _____ after adjectives.

2 After nouns or pronouns, use _____ to show purpose.

3 It's common to use _____ after expressions like *spend / waste time* and *have (no) fun*.

B ▶ **Now go to page 135. Look at the grammar chart and do the grammar exercise for 7.1.**

C Circle the correct options and complete the sentences with your own ideas. Then compare your sentences with a group. Whose ideas were the most unusual?

1 It's unusual *to see / seeing* …

2 I often waste time *to do / doing* …

3 … is an interesting subject *to study / studying*.

4 I need someone *to give / giving* me advice about …

5 I usually feel nervous *to wait / waiting* to …

4 SPEAKING

A **PAIR WORK** Talk about your job or a job you'd like to have. Explain what satisfaction you (would) get out of it. Compare your thoughts with your partner's.

> As a hairdresser, I get **a chance to meet** a lot of people. I feel that I can **make a difference** for my customers. It's **not** always **easy to get** things just right, but when you succeed, it's really rewarding.

7.2 BUYER'S REGRET

LESSON OBJECTIVE
■ talk about purchases

1 LANGUAGE IN CONTEXT

A   PAIR WORK   THINK CRITICALLY   Do you read product reviews when you're deciding to buy an item online? Do they influence your purchase? What other factors influence your purchase?

B   Read the reviews. What did each person buy, and why? Why were the people dissatisfied? What do you think Dan did next?

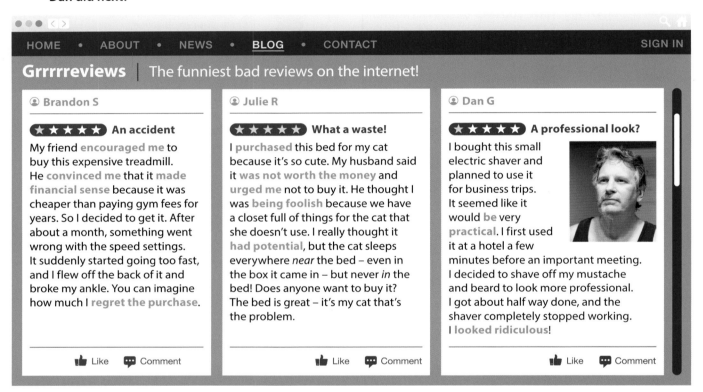

HOME • ABOUT • NEWS • **BLOG** • CONTACT   SIGN IN

Grrrrreviews | The funniest bad reviews on the internet!

⊕ Brandon S

★★★★★ **An accident**

My friend **encouraged me** to buy this expensive treadmill. He **convinced me** that it **made financial sense** because it was cheaper than paying gym fees for years. So I decided to get it. After about a month, something went wrong with the speed settings. It suddenly started going too fast, and I flew off the back of it and broke my ankle. You can imagine how much I **regret the purchase**.

👍 Like   💬 Comment

⊕ Julie R

★★★★★ **What a waste!**

I **purchased** this bed for my cat because it's so cute. My husband said it **was not worth the money** and **urged me** not to buy it. He thought I was **being foolish** because we have a closet full of things for the cat that she doesn't use. I really thought it **had potential**, but the cat sleeps everywhere *near* the bed – even in the box it came in – but never *in* the bed! Does anyone want to buy it? The bed is great – it's my cat that's the problem.

👍 Like   💬 Comment

⊕ Dan G

★★★★★ **A professional look?**

I bought this small electric shaver and planned to use it for business trips. It seemed like it would **be** very **practical**. I first used it at a hotel a few minutes before an important meeting. I decided to shave off my mustache and beard to look more professional. I got about half way done, and the shaver completely stopped working. I **looked ridiculous**!

👍 Like   💬 Comment

C   PAIR WORK   THINK CRITICALLY   Read again. Which of these reviews would you have found most helpful? Why? In general, which are more helpful: good or bad product reviews? What kind of information do you find most useful?

2 VOCABULARY: Making purchases

FIND IT

A   🔊 **2.04** Look at the expressions in the box. What items are they associated with in the product reviews? Which one is not in the text? What do the expressions mean? Use a dictionary or your phone to help you. Then listen and check the definitions.

be foolish	be practical	convince sb (to do sth)	encourage sb (to do sth)
have appeal	have potential	look ridiculous	make financial sense
not be worth the money	purchase sth	regret a/the purchase	urge sb (to do sth)

B   ▶ Now go to page 147. Do the vocabulary exercises for 7.2.

C   GROUP WORK   Talk about a bad purchase you've made. What was it? Why do you regret buying it?

3 GRAMMAR: Infinitives after verbs with and without objects

A Read the sentences in the grammar box. (Circle) the correct option to answer the question.

> ### Infinitives after verbs with and without objects
>
> My friend **encouraged me to buy** this expensive treadmill.
>
> My husband … **urged me not to buy** it.
>
> Does anyone **want to buy** it?
>
> I … **planned to use** it for business trips.

When is the subject of the main verb and the subject of the infinitive different?

a With verbs followed directly by an infinitive, without an object

b When there's an object between the main verb and the infinitive

B ▶ **Now go to page 135. Look at the grammar chart and do the grammar exercise for 7.2.**

C **Change the sentences below so that they are true for you. Add one more sentence to each statement using the words in parentheses or your own ideas. Use infinitives in each sentence. Check your accuracy. Then share your sentences with a partner. Did you have similar ideas?**

1 My friends often offer to lend me some money. (like)

My parents often offer to lend me some money, but I don't like to borrow from them.

2 I'd like my brother to help me choose a new phone. (advise)

3 My mother expects me to help her with her shopping. (persuade)

4 My manager agreed not to give me so much work. (promise)

5 I hate ads that encourage you to lose weight. (tell)

> ✔ **ACCURACY** CHECK
>
> Remember to use an object or object pronoun after verbs like *encourage, persuade,* and *urge.*
>
> *The ad* ~~encouraged to buy~~ *new sunglasses.* ✗
> *The ad encouraged me to buy new sunglasses.* ✓

4 SPEAKING

A PAIR WORK **Tell your partner about things you've bought for each of these categories. Why did you buy them? Were they worthwhile purchases? Use verbs + infinitives.**

clothing   furniture   sports gear   technology   transportation

My friend **persuaded me to buy** a scooter because it **made financial sense** at the time.

B PAIR WORK **Choose an item you talked about in exercise 4A and write a short review. Exchange your reviews with a partner. Do you want to buy the product? Why or why not?**

A GOOD BARGAIN

1 LISTENING

A Is bargaining (= trying to get a lower price) common in your culture? What kinds of things do people bargain for?

B 🔊 **2.05** Listen. Sergio is studying abroad for a year and wants to buy a desk at a street market for his room. What price does the seller want at first? What is their final agreement?

C 🔊 **2.05** **UNDERSTAND PERSUASIVE TECHNIQUES**
Listen again. Check (✓) the techniques Sergio and Megan use to get the best deal.

1 Sergio: ☐ points out some problems with the desk
☐ is prepared to walk away
☐ refuses to buy the desk without the chair
☐ pretends he doesn't have a way to get it home

2 Megan: ☐ says the desk was never used
☐ says she'll give Sergio the chair for free
☐ says the desk is not too old
☐ says she'll deliver the desk for free

INSIDER ENGLISH

you bet = certainly, I'd be happy to

D **GROUP WORK** **THINK CRITICALLY** Can you add any more techniques to the list above? In your country, what do buyers and sellers do to get the best price when bargaining? Discuss and then describe a bargaining experience you or someone you know had. How successful was it?

2 PRONUNCIATION: Listening for vowel linking between words

A 🔊 **2.06** Listen to how the underlined words link.

It's <u>only a</u> few years old.   Can you <u>go any</u> lower?

B 🔊 **2.07** <u>Underline</u> the linked words in the sentences below and write whether there is a sound like /j/ or /w/ between them.

How much are you asking?   Would you be willing to accept $125?

How about $120?   I'll walk around and see if …

C Ⓒircle the correct option to complete the sentences.

When a word ends with a /uː/ or /iː/ and the next word begins with a *consonant / vowel*, there is usually linking. If the first word ends in /iː/, /eɪ/, /aɪ/, or /ɔɪ/, there is a linking sound like /j/. If the first word ends in /uː/, /oʊ/, or /aʊ/, there is a linking sound like /w/.

3 SPEAKING SKILLS

A 🔊 **2.05** **PAIR WORK** Look at these expressions from the conversation in exercise 1B on page 70. Which ones are used for (a) accepting an offer, (b) bargaining, or (c) rejecting an offer? Write *a*, *b*, or *c* next to each one. Then say which expressions can be used by the buyer, the seller, or both. Where do you think vowel linking occurs in these expressions? Listen to the conversation again to check.

Negotiate a price

1 So, how much are you asking for … ? _____
2 That's a little on the high side. Can you go any lower? _____
3 I'm sorry, but I can't accept that. _____
4 Would you be willing to accept … ? _____
5 Sorry, but no deal. _____
6 $… is the best I can do. _____
7 Sorry, but I don't think it's worth that much. _____
8 I'll throw … in for free. _____
9 That's my final offer. _____
10 That sounds fair enough. _____
11 I think I can accept that. _____
12 You've got a deal. _____

B **PAIR WORK** Choose the role of a buyer or a seller. Role play a conversation using the prompts below and expressions from exercise 3A.

Buyer   You are interested in a product. Ask the price.
Seller   Suggest a price and praise the product.
Buyer   Say the price is too high and point out a fault.
Seller   Reject the offer.
Buyer   Offer an alternative price.
Seller   Accept the offer.

4 PRONUNCIATION: Saying /ŋ/

A 🔊 **2.08** Listen and underline the /ŋ/ sounds.

1 Is this the computer you're selling?
2 Would you be willing to accept less?
3 My uncle was angry because I went shopping.
4 There's always a danger of paying too much for something.

B 🔊 **2.09** Write the word with /ŋ/ next to the definition. Then listen to check your work and repeat the words with /ŋ/.

1 _____ – the muscle in your mouth
2 _____ – fast walking
3 _____ – it connects your foot and leg
4 _____ – the opposite of "answering"
5 _____ – your mother's brother
6 _____ – the sound babies make when they are uncomfortable or unhappy

C **GROUP WORK** Make your own quiz as in exercise 4B, where all the answers are words with /ŋ/. Then groups exchange quizzes and say the words, focusing on the pronunciation of /ŋ/.

5 SPEAKING

A **PAIR WORK** Student A: Go to page 158. Student B: Go to page 159. Follow the instructions.

7.4 MONEY'S WORTH

LESSON OBJECTIVE
- write a for-and-against essay

1 READING

A **PAIR WORK** What kind of things do you enjoy spending money on? Why?

B **IDENTIFY MAIN POINTS** Read the article. What are the main ideas of the sections "The Problem with Possessions" and "The Power of Experiences"?

Why you should spend your money on experiences, not things

When you work hard every single day and there's only so much money left after your regular expenses, you have to make sure you spend it well. So spend it on what science says will make you happy.

The problem with possessions

A 20-year study by Dr. Thomas Gilovich, a psychology professor at Cornell University, reached a powerful conclusion: Don't spend your money on things. The trouble with things is that the happiness they provide goes away quickly. There are three important reasons for this:

> What seemed unusual and exciting at first quickly becomes normal.

> As soon as we get used to a new possession, we look for an even better one.

> We buy something and are thrilled with it until a friend buys a better one – and there's always someone with a better one.

The power of experiences

Gilovich and other researchers have found that experiences – as short as they may be – bring happiness that lasts longer than things. Here's why:

1 Experiences become a part of our identity. We are not our possessions, but we *are* the combination of everything we've seen, the things we've done, and the places we've been. Buying the newest phone isn't going to change who you are, but hiking across a mountain range from start to finish definitely will.

2 Anticipation is important. Gilovich also studied anticipation and found that anticipation of an experience causes excitement and enjoyment, while anticipation of getting a possession causes impatience. Experiences are enjoyable from the very first moments of planning all the way through to the memories you appreciate forever.

3 Experiences don't last (which is a good thing). Have you ever bought something that wasn't as beneficial as you thought it would be? Once you buy it, it's right there in your face, reminding you of your disappointment. And even if an item does meet your expectations, it's common to regret the purchase: "Sure, it's cool, but it probably wasn't worth the money." We don't do that with experiences. The fact that they last for only a short time is part of what makes them worthwhile, and that value tends to increase as time passes.

Adapted from an article by Travis Bradberry, PhD, on the Talentsmart website.

GLOSSARY
anticipation (*n*) a feeling of excitement about something that is going to happen

C **IDENTIFY SUPPORTING DETAILS** Write the number of the section from the article (1–3) for each supporting detail. If the supporting detail is not in the article, write *X*.

Experiences …

a help us gain confidence and overcome problems. _____

b aren't compared as often as things. _____

c define and change who we are. _____

d cause more excitement than possessions. _____

e can be more expensive than possessions. _____

f add value to our lives that can last a lifetime. _____

D **GROUP WORK** **THINK CRITICALLY** Think of more ideas <u>in favor of</u> buying experiences instead of things. Then think of ideas <u>against</u> buying experiences. Which do you agree with more?

2 WRITING

A **Read part of an essay on the value of possessions. What two arguments are given? What's the author's opinion?**

How Valuable Are Our Possessions?

Recently, there have been a number of articles about the value of experiences in comparison with possessions. The writers have described various ways in which experiences are more beneficial and … . Others, however, disagree and … .

Let us consider some arguments in favor of possessions. To begin with, we can keep our possessions, unlike experiences, which only last a short time. We can share … . Valuable possessions can give us a sense of … For example, … . Another advantage is that possessions can have a sentimental value. For instance, … .

On the other hand, there are a number of arguments that challenge the value of possessions. First, although some possessions contribute to our comfort, many are unnecessary and take up a lot of space. Yet we often find it hard to part with them. A lot of people … . Another disadvantage is possessions make us competitive. For example, … . In addition, … .

Overall, I believe that possessions make a great contribution to our lives. Even though there are problems associated with them, they make our day-to-day life more enjoyable and represent a part of who we are.

B **ORGANIZE AN ESSAY** **Read about how to write a for-and-against essay. Match the paragraph types in the box with their descriptions.**

> Against   Conclusion   For   Introduction

A for-and-against essay is a formal piece of writing in which you write about a topic from opposite points of view. It often has four paragraphs:

1 _____ : Present the topic but don't give your opinion about it.
2 _____ : Give two or three arguments in favor of the topic with examples or reasons.
3 _____ : Give two or three arguments against the topic with examples or reasons.
4 _____ : Give your opinion. Say why you find one side more convincing than the other.

REGISTER CHECK

Let us is often used in formal writing. *Let's* is used in less formal writing or when speaking.

C **PAIR WORK** **Which useful expressions below does the author use in the essay in exercise 2A? With a partner think of ideas that could complete the essay.**

> **Useful expressions**
>
> **Listing:** First, To begin with, Second, Finally, One/Another advantage/disadvantage is
> **Adding:** In addition, Furthermore, as well as
> **Contrasting:** On the other hand, However, Nevertheless, Nonetheless, Even though
> **Giving examples:** For example, For instance, such as
> **Concluding:** In conclusion, To sum up, Overall (*followed by* it is my opinion that), I think/believe that

WRITE IT

D **PLAN** **You're going to write a for-and-against essay. Choose one of the following subjects:**

a How Valuable Are Experiences?
b How Valuable Are Our Possessions?

With a partner, brainstorm some ideas for the essay. Then decide what you'll include in each paragraph from exercise 2B.

E **Write your essay. Make sure you use some of the useful expressions from exercise 2C.**

F **PAIR WORK** **Exchange essays with a partner. Did you choose the same subject? Are your conclusions the same?**

7.5 TIME TO SPEAK
Bargain boat trip

A Look at the pictures. Which boat trip would you prefer to go on? Who would you go with? Discuss your reasons with a partner.

B DISCUSS You and a group of friends won a boat trip and beach party. The trip and activities are free, but you have to pay for extras. In pairs, look at the information from the boat company. Discuss which activities and which extras you want in order to make the day worthwhile. How much will the extras cost?

C DECIDE Your group's budget is $500. Compare it with the cost of the extras from part B. Decide what you need to do to stay within your budget. You can remove or add extras. Also, plan how to bargain with the boat company. Which prices do you think are too expensive or unfair and can be negotiated?

D PREPARE Talk with your partner about how you could negotiate a better deal. Explain why you believe your strategy could be successful.

E AGREE Work with another pair. One pair is the friends and the other is the boat company. Negotiate a deal. Then change roles and repeat.

F PRESENT Tell the class which activities you're going to do and which extras you agreed on. The class chooses the best trip.

To check your progress, go to page 155.

Beach cruise

River cruise

City cruise

PRICE LIST

Cost for a 2-hour boat tour for 25 people + 3-hour beach stop

Beach activities (choose two):
- beach volleyball
- parasailing
- dance party with a DJ
- live concert
- surfing lessons
- snorkeling

Extras (cost for entire group)
+ sodas on the boat	$50
+ cold food on the boat	$100
+ sodas on the beach	$100
+ cold food on the beach	$200
or barbecued food on the beach	$300
+ beach chairs	$100
+ beach umbrellas	$100
+ cancellation insurance (for bad weather)	$50

USEFUL PHRASES

DISCUSS

It looks like … is a really good value …

If I have to choose between … and … ,

I'd rather … than …

Having … would make a real difference.

PREPARE

We could ask them to combine … and …

We should pay for … and see if they'll throw in … for free.

Let's see if they'd be willing to accept $… for …

That might work because …

They can't say no to …

UNIT OBJECTIVES
- talk about neatness and messiness
- talk about side projects
- suggest and show interest in ideas
- write a complaint letter
- make a podcast on ways to reduce stress

SMALL THINGS MATTER

8

START SPEAKING

A **What can you tell about the person who works here? What objects were used to make the work area more practical and personalized?**

B **How do you make your work area more practical? How do you personalize it?**

C **In what other areas of your life can you use small things to make them more pleasant or personal (e.g., wallpaper on your phone)? How do these items make a difference? How do they make you feel? Tell your partner. For ideas, watch Jacqueline's video.**

EXPERT SPEAKER

Are any of Jacqueline's examples similar to yours?

ANNOYING LITTLE THINGS

1 LANGUAGE IN CONTEXT

A **PAIR WORK** Think about the best thing about growing up in your family home. Tell your partner what your family does that you love and appreciate. What little things do they do that annoy you?

B 🔊 **2.10** In an episode of a TV show called *You Should Talk!*, family members talk about living with each other. Read and listen. What annoying habits do Nicole and Paul have?

🔊 **2.10 Audio script**

Host	So, Nicole and Paul, who's more **disorganized**?
Paul	Definitely Nicole. Like, the other night, we were supposed to meet some friends at seven, and Nicole was going to drive us. We were about to leave the house, but she couldn't find her keys – as *usual*. We normally **hang them up** on the wall by the front door.
Nicole	Yeah, Paul likes to **line up** all the keys from the biggest to the smallest. He also **puts his books in alphabetical order**, and his desk **is** always **organized** with all his office stuff …
Paul	OK, OK, but we're talking about you right now. Her keys were bound to be in the house somewhere, so we were forced to go room by room looking for them. Eventually she found them. They **were tangled up** with some earphones in the pocket of some jeans. Unbelievable!
Nicole	You should talk! At least my jeans were in the closet – unlike your shoes!
Host	Wait. A minute ago, you were saying how Paul **arranges keys and books neatly**. And now I'm hearing he **leaves his shoes all over the place**?
Nicole	Yes! I mean, they're not all **jumbled up**. They're sure to be neatly placed side by side on the floor, but they're everywhere!
Paul	At least I don't **throw** my clothes **on** the floor, like some people I know. I **fold them** neatly and **put them in a pile** on the chair by my bed.
Nicole	Yeah. Even when he doesn't **put things away**, he does it neatly!

C 🔊 **2.10** **PAIR WORK** **THINK CRITICALLY** Read and listen again. Who would you find more annoying to live with? Why do you think people get annoyed over small, silly things? What compromises do we need to make when living with other people?

INSIDER ENGLISH

Say *You should talk* to mean "You are guilty of the same behavior you have just criticized."

2 VOCABULARY: Describing neatness and messiness

A 🔊 **2.11** Look at the expressions in **bold** in the text. Which do we use to talk about things that are neat, messy, or both? Copy the chart and complete it. Then listen and check your work.

Neat	Messy	Both

B ▶ Now go to page 148. Do the vocabulary exercises for 8.1.

C **PAIR WORK** What expressions from the box can you use to describe yourself? Which ones can you use to describe the person or people you live with? Can you give some example situations to illustrate?

3 GRAMMAR: Modal-like expressions with *be*

A **Read the sentences in the grammar box. Match the expressions (1–4) to the descriptions (a–d).**

> **Modal-like expressions with *be***
>
> We **were supposed to** meet some friends at seven.
>
> We **were about to** leave the house, but she couldn't find her keys.
>
> Her keys **were bound to** be in the house somewhere.
>
> We **were forced to** go room by room looking for them.
>
> They**'re sure to** be neatly placed side by side on the floor.

1 be supposed to ____
2 be about to ____
3 be bound to / be sure to ____
4 be forced to ____

a be made to do something we don't want to
b be certain to do something or to happen
c be expected to happen because it was arranged
d be going to do something very soon

B ▶ **Now go to page 136. Look at the grammar chart and do the grammar exercise for 8.1.**

C **Imagine you have a terrible roommate who is messy and disorganized. Make a list of complaints about him or her using modal-like expressions with *be*, the prompts, and some ideas of your own. Then compare with a partner. Whose roommate is more annoying?**

1 not wiping feet when it rains

   He's sure to walk in without wiping his feet, so I'm forced to clean up the muddy floor.

2 putting away clean dishes
3 cleaning up after a party
4 throwing towels on the floor
5 losing keys to the apartment

4 SPEAKING

A **PAIR WORK** **Imagine the terrible roommate you described in exercise 3C is gone, and you are looking for a new one. With a partner, try to agree on some house rules for your future roommate.**

> OK, first, pay your rent on time. Second, **hang up** your clothes. Don't **leave them all over the place**.

> Yeah, and don't just **throw the dishes in** the sink. Wash them right away, or they**'re bound** to smell bad.

8.2 SIDE PROJECTS

1 LANGUAGE IN CONTEXT

A   Look at the title of Max's blog. What do you think it means? Then read the blog. What's (1) a side project, (2) Kyle's side project, (3) Max's side project?

HOME   ABOUT   **BLOG**   CONTACT US

LIVING YOUR DREAMS (On the side)

by FilmGuyMax

My friend Kyle

Do you have a side project? You know, the thing you do that isn't your real job but you do it because you love it? Side projects are often creative, but they're more than a hobby. My friend Kyle, for example, is a mechanic, and in his free time he repairs old bikes for a kids' charity. It's work, but not work. He does it because he **thoroughly** enjoys it. And that's the great thing about a side project. It *won't* cause you stress but *will* give you a real sense of satisfaction. And unlike a job, you can usually do things **at your own pace** and **on your own time**.

I'm a film studies student, and my side project is making a documentary about college. I'm filming it **little by little**, and eventually I'm going to edit it into an hour-long show. It'll be a surprise for my friends because I'm not showing it to them until it's done. But this side project has another purpose. In a couple of years, I'll be looking for a job, and this video is going to be a useful example of my skills as a filmmaker. If things go **smoothly**, I might start my own video production business one day. So, as I work on my video, I'll also be moving **steadily** toward that goal. But if things don't go **as expected**, at least I'll have a nice souvenir of my college years.

B   Read the blog again. What are the benefits of a side project? How will Max's side project be useful to him?

C   PAIR WORK   What side projects do you or the people you know have? Do you think they will help you to achieve your dreams?

2 VOCABULARY: Talking about progress

FIND IT

A   🔊 2.12   PAIR WORK   Look at the expressions in the box. What do they mean? Use a dictionary, your phone, or the context in the blog to help you. Which were used in the blog post? Which ones have a similar meaning? Then listen to the definitions and check your work.

as expected	at my own pace	effectively	efficiently
little by little	on my own time	smoothly	steadily
successfully	thoroughly	with difficulty	with ease

B   ▶ Now go to page 148. Do the vocabulary exercises for 8.2.

C   PAIR WORK   THINK CRITICALLY   Compare main occupations with side projects. What are their pros and cons? What are the differences in (a) how we work on them and (b) how we feel about them?

3 GRAMMAR: Future forms

A Read the sentences in the grammar box. Circle the correct options to complete the rules.

> **Future forms**
>
> It **won't cause** you stress but **will give** you a real sense of satisfaction.
> Eventually I'**m going to edit** it.
> I'**m not showing** it to them until it's done.
> In a couple of years, I'**ll be looking for** a job.
> This video **is going to be** a useful example of my skills as a filmmaker.
> If things go smoothly, I **might start** my own video production business one day.

1 Use *be going to*, *will*, or **don't / won't** for predictions, expectations, or guesses about the future.

2 Use *be going to* or the **present continuous / simple present** for future plans and intentions.

3 Use *will + be +* verb *+ -ing* for **an action in progress / a finished action** at a time in the future.

4 Use *might*, *may*, or *could* when you're **certain / uncertain** about the future.

B ▶ **Now go to page 136. Look at the grammar chart and do the grammar exercise for 8.2.**

C Write six sentences on plans and predictions about your work, studies, or side projects. Use a different future form from exercise 3A in each sentence. Check your accuracy. Then compare with a partner. Are any of your predictions similar?

 ACCURACY CHECK

Use the future continuous, not the present continuous, for an action in progress in the future.

In a couple of years, I'm looking for a job. ✗
In a couple of years, I'll be looking for a job. ✓

4 SPEAKING

A **PAIR WORK** Choose a side project from the list below or your own idea. Think about how it will fit with your short-term and long-term plans, ambitions, or goals. Is it linked to your career in any way? Then tell each other about your side project. Ask questions to find out more. For ideas, watch Jacqueline's video.

create an app	do a podcast	grow plants
improve your cooking skills	make jewelry or furniture	play in a band
start an English speaking group	write a blog	write a children's book

I'm studying to become a teacher, but my side project is learning to play the guitar. Right now, I'm practicing the basics **little by little**, but in several months, I'll **be successfully playing** songs. Maybe I **could** even **be** a guitar teacher someday. It'**s going to be** fun!

EXPERT SPEAKER

Is Jacqueline's side project something you'd ever do? Why or why not?

THE LITTLE TOUCHES

1 LISTENING

A 🔊 2.13 [PAIR WORK] **Look at the pictures. What kind of event do you think the items in picture A would be good for? What can you see in picture B? Are you sure? Then listen to a podcast about event planning and check your answers.**

B 🔊 2.13 [RECOGNIZE EMPHASIS] **Listen again. The speakers emphasize the following words. Does the emphasis for each word (a) show a contrasting idea or (b) mean *very*?**

1 and small ____
2 awesome ____
3 complex ____
4 the birthday girl ____
5 such ____
6 really ____

C 🔊 2.13 [PAIR WORK] [THINK CRITICALLY] **Listen again. What ideas do the speakers have for "little touches"? Do you like the ideas? What kind of things, do you think, make events special and memorable? What kind of things are not worth the trouble? Why?**

2 PRONUNCIATION: Listening for emphasis

A 🔊 2.14 **Listen to the emphasis on the underlined words.**

Plan all types of events – big <u>and</u> small   That's an <u>awesome</u> idea.   Or it can be a <u>complex</u> theme like travel.

B 🔊 2.15 **Listen and <u>underline</u> the words that are emphasized.**

1 Well, the birthday girl loved it, but not everyone likes strawberries.
2 That's such a terrific idea.
3 And it really is the little things they remember.

C **Circle the correct options to complete the sentences.**

When we want to show emphasis, we put the main stress on the word we want to emphasize. We usually do this by using a *higher* / *lower* pitch on this word. The main stress *can* / *cannot* include functional words like determiners.

3 SPEAKING SKILLS

A 🔊 **2.13** **Complete the expressions from the conversation in exercise 1B on page 80. Then decide if they are used to suggest an idea or to show interest in an idea. Write *S* (suggest) or *Sh* (show). Listen to the podcast again to check.**

Suggest and show interest in ideas

1 One/Another _____ you/we can do is … _____	**5** I _____ everyone loved / will love that! _____
2 That's _____ a terrific / an awesome idea. _____	**6** It never _____ to … _____
3 What a _____ idea! _____	**7** That's always _____ considering. _____
4 … always goes _____ well. _____	**8** … is a good _____ to approach it. _____

B │ PAIR WORK │ **You're planning a small summer party for your classmates. Complete the conversation with your own ideas. Then compare with another pair. Which of their ideas would you like to use?**

A Do you have any ideas for the party?

B Well, I think ¹ _____ is a good way to approach it. Actually, ² _____ always goes over well.

A That's ³ _____ idea. Also, it never hurts to ⁴ _____.

B True, and another thing we can do is ⁵ _____.

A Yeah, that's always worth considering. And how about ⁶ _____?

4 PRONUNCIATION: Saying words that show a contrast

A 🔊 **2.16** **Listen to the recording. Can you hear the pitch change on one key word in each sentence? Underline these words.**

1 I bet everyone loved that!

2 Well, most people did.

3 Her birthday's not in March, it's in April.

B 🔊 **2.17** **Underline the words that show a contrast. Listen and check your work. Then repeat the sentences.**

1 It wasn't her birthday, it was his.

2 I don't have any ideas, but Diego does.

3 Shall we get a present or give her some money?

4 He didn't just like it, he loved it!

C │ PAIR WORK │ **One student says a sentence. The other replies with a contrast.**

1 Let's drive to the party.
   No, we'll walk. ↘

2 We'll celebrate at home.

3 Tom will be late.

4 Wasn't she wearing the red dress?

5 The party finishes at ten.

5 SPEAKING

FIND IT

A │ GROUP WORK │ **You are planning an event together. Choose an idea in the box. Talk about the theme, music, decorations, and food you'll have. Include little touches to make the event special. You can check online for ideas.**

a birthday party for a child	a company dinner
a family reunion	a graduation party

B **Describe your plan to the class. Which is the most entertaining?**

*OK, let's plan a company dinner. I think choosing an interesting theme **is a good way to approach it**.*

*OK, well, a beach theme **always goes over well. One thing we can do is** give everyone sunglasses to wear.*

1   READING

A   **Have you ever made a formal complaint? What was the problem? Was your complaint effective?**

B   **IDENTIFY WRITER'S PURPOSE** **Read the article. What's its purpose? What specific examples of customer problems does the writer mention? Which are valid reasons for complaints?**

Do you have a problem with a product, service, or company? It might be time to make a formal complaint. Anna Tims, a writer who focuses on consumer affairs, offers a list of tips for successful complaining. The secret is getting a lot of small things right.

HOW TO COMPLAIN EFFECTIVELY

Most large companies get hundreds of complaints – some silly and some serious. No matter how important your complaint is to you, it will just be added to a pile of complaints that a stressed-out customer service worker needs to read. So to be sure it makes the biggest impact, you must know how to state your complaint effectively. Follow these steps, and you're bound to get your problems solved.

☑ MAKE SURE YOUR COMPLAINT IS VALID
Your concern needs to be realistic. For example, if fees for ending a cell phone service contract early stop you from going to a cheaper cell phone service provider, that's too bad. You should have understood the contract. If, however, you have received poor service, you have the right to end your contract early. Or if you dropped your product and then stepped on it accidentally, it's your fault. But if a product breaks when you set it down gently, it's sure to be faulty.

☑ FIGURE OUT WHAT YOU WANT TO ACHIEVE
Do you want a refund, a replacement, or simply an apology? If you want a refund, you have to act quickly or you might lose your right to one. If you complain by phone, make a note of who you spoke to and when, and follow up the call with a letter restating your complaint and the response you got on the phone. Do the same if you sent the complaint through the company's website, so you have a record of it.

☑ ALWAYS ADDRESS A LETTER TO A SPECIFIC PERSON
It is best to start with the customer service manager. (If you aim too high – for example, the company president – you will be waiting while your letter is passed around until it reaches the right person.) Find out the manager's name and use their full title – Dr., Mr., Mrs., or Ms. A little thing like using someone's name can make a big impression.

☑ INCLUDE YOUR DETAILS
Remember to include your full name, address, and any order or reference numbers near the top of the letter. If a company can't easily find you in their system, they may not respond.

☑ KEEP COPIES
Make copies of all relevant documents – such as receipts, bank statements, order forms, and advertisements – and include them to support your complaint. If you want a new but stained couch replaced, include a photo of the damage.

☑ CHECK YOUR SPELLING
Carelessly written letters suggest you are as sloppy as the company you are complaining about.

☑ BE POLITE AND REASONABLE
Whether you are writing or calling, stay calm. Anger will give companies an excuse to refuse to deal with you.

☑ NAME NAMES
If you mention the unhelpful attitude of, for example, a store manager or customer service representative, try to include their names.

☑ SET A DEADLINE
Give the company a deadline for sending a useful response – 14 days is fair. Make a note of the date so you can increase the pressure if it is missed.

☑ MAKE SURE YOUR COMPLAINT ARRIVES
Send all letters by certified mail or special delivery so the company can't deny receiving them. If you use email, ask the person to confirm once they get it.

Adapted from an article by Anna Tims in The Guardian

GLOSSARY
consumer affairs (*n*) a system related to protecting people who buy products and services
faulty (*adj*) not perfectly made or does not work correctly
sloppy (*adj*) not being careful or making an effort

C   **Read the article again. Which points apply to (1) both a complaint letter and a phone call and (2) only a complaint letter?**

D   **PAIR WORK** **THINK CRITICALLY** **Which three points in the article do you think would be the most effective? Why? Are there any points that won't have an effect? Why not?**

2 WRITING

A   Read Karen's letter to the customer service manager of Markus Appliances. What's the problem? Why is she not happy with the sales manager's response? What does she want?

Reply   Forward

To: Mr. Edwards
From: Karen Rebecca Mason
Subject: RE: Faulty SUPERWASH Washing Machine, model number RGM205

Dear Mr. Edwards,

I am writing to complain about the above washing machine, which I bought during your Summer Sale on July 15. I purchased it for $175.99 at the Main Street branch of Markus Appliances and include a copy of the receipt as proof of purchase.

After the machine was delivered, I tried to use it, but it wouldn't turn on. I checked the connection, which was fine, but the machine had no power. I immediately returned to the store and explained the problem to the sales manager, Rob Clark. At first, he suggested there was something wrong with the power in my house. When I insisted that the machine was faulty, he said, "Sorry, but you bought it during the half-price sale. We don't accept the return of sale items."

I find this unacceptable. First, the item is obviously faulty. Second, your company advertisement (copy included) states that you accept all returns without question. I believe that includes sale items. Third, I feel Mr. Clark should be friendlier. It's a small thing, but a smile goes a long way.

I would like your company to pick up the washing machine from my house and send me a refund of $175.99. I look forward to hearing from you within the next ten days.

Sincerely,

Karen Rebecca Mason

REGISTER CHECK

In formal written complaints, we often use expressions like *I find, I feel, I believe,* or *I think* to make statements less direct and more polite.

Direct

This is unacceptable.
Mr. Clark should be friendlier.

Less direct

I find this unacceptable.
I feel Mr. Clark should be friendlier.

B   **PAIR WORK**   **THINK CRITICALLY**   Which of the tips in the article in exercise 1A on page 82 did Karen follow?

C   **AVOID RUN-ON SENTENCES AND SENTENCE FRAGMENTS**   Read about two kinds of sentences to avoid in more formal writing. Look at the examples below. How could the sentences be improved? Then find good versions of each in Karen's letter in exercise 2A.

Run-on sentences (They go on and on.)

1   I am writing to complain about the above washing machine, which I bought during your Summer Sale on July 15 for $175.99 at the Main Street branch of Markus Appliances and for which I include a copy of the receipt as proof of purchase.

Sentence fragments (Incomplete sentences)

2   Went back to the store. Explained problem to sales manager Rob Clark.

3   Unacceptable. First, obviously faulty.

WRITE IT

D   **PLAN**   You're going to write a complaint letter. Choose an idea in the box or something you experienced yourself. With a partner, describe the problem and how you want the company to solve it. Then look at the letter in exercise 2A. What type of information should each paragraph contain in a complaint letter? How will you start and end the letter?

| a bad restaurant meal | a broken or faulty item or package |
| poor customer service | an item that's different from the advertisement |

E   Write your complaint letter.

F   **PAIR WORK**   Exchange your letters of complaint. How effective is your partner's letter?

TIME TO SPEAK
The key to less stress

NOT STRESSED AT ALL **VERY STRESSED**

A **DISCUSS** How stressed are you? Where would you put yourself on the scale above? Would you say most of your stress is caused by one or two big things or a number of small things? In pairs, discuss examples of big and small things that can make you feel stressed. For ideas look at the pictures. Add four ideas of your own.

B Compare your ideas with other pairs. Find out common causes of stress.

C **DECIDE** Which of the causes of stress from part B can be reduced by taking simple actions? What actions can be taken? With your partner from part A, discuss the ideas in the box and your own ideas. Then choose your top three effective and simple actions.

> **SIMPLE ACTIONS TO REDUCE STRESS:**
>
> | | | |
> |---|---|---|
> | Delete it. | Don't read it. | Don't reply. |
> | Make "to-do" lists. | Do it right away. | Get up earlier. |
> | Go to bed later. | Say "No!" | Discuss the problem. |

D **PREPARE** You're going to present your actions in a short podcast. Plan: (1) the introduction, (2) your actions and the reasons why you think they're simple and effective (give some examples), and (3) the conclusion. You can take notes.

E **PRESENT** Present your podcast to the class. Answer any questions about it.

F **AGREE** The class compares the podcasts and chooses two that have the best ideas and are well presented.

To check your progress, go to page 155.

USEFUL PHRASES

DECIDE

One/Another thing you could do is …

It never hurts to …

… is always worth considering.

… is a good way to approach it.

PREPARE

If you do this, you're bound to / sure to …

You're going to …

You might …

You'll be + verb + -ing …

UNIT OBJECTIVES
■ talk about how your life might be different
■ talk about mistakes
■ reassure someone about a problem
■ write an article giving tips
■ talk about key events in your life

THINGS HAPPEN

9

START SPEAKING

A   **Look at the picture. What do you think the man expected to be doing that day? What happened instead? How could this situation develop?**

B   **Think of a situation when something very unexpected completely changed your plans. What happened? Was the change for the better or worse?**

C   **Do you believe in chance? Or are the best things that happen to us always planned? Discuss some examples. For ideas, watch Carolina's video.**

EXPERT SPEAKER

Have you ever had an experience similar to Carolina's?

9.1 TURNING POINTS

1 LANGUAGE IN CONTEXT

A **PAIR WORK** What is fate? Do you believe in it?

B Read the online posts. What is each person's opinion about luck?

X-ray technician

Comments   Account   Sign out

Lara_Park   *posted 2 days ago*
Do you believe in **fate**? My brother says there's no such thing. But I think everything happens for a reason, and there are no **coincidences**. When you look back on your life, you can see the **path** that has led to your life today. For example, I was studying finance and wanted to go into banking. Then my brother accidentally slammed the car door on my finger – ouch! The doctor sent me for an X-ray, which was SO COOL! I could see my own bones on the screen, and the X-ray tech explained everything and answered all my questions. Totally fascinating! If I could find her, I'd thank her because that was a **life-changing experience**. I dropped finance and enrolled in a radiology course. Now, I say that was fate. I mean, if my brother hadn't broken my finger, I wouldn't be an X-ray technician today. But he says it was just a **lucky break**! (Ha! That's a good one.)
   Like   Comment

PracticalGal   *posted 2 days ago*
I agree with your brother. People make **deliberate decisions** based on current circumstances, even if that's just a **chance encounter**. If you hadn't met that X-ray tech, you might have learned about radiology some other way. But you weren't unhappy in finance, so even if you were a banker now, you'd still be happy.
   Like   Comment

Jace_the_Ace   *posted 2 days ago*
I think life is a combination of luck and **determination**. Sometimes, like Lara, you**'re in the right place at the right time**, but it takes hard work and skill to turn luck into a real opportunity.
   Like   Comment

C Read the posts again. What events led to Lara's job?

D **GROUP WORK** **THINK CRITICALLY** Say whose opinion you agree with the most. Then talk about someone who played a part in any of your life-changing experiences.

2 VOCABULARY: Luck and choice

A 🔊 **2.18** Which expressions in the box are about luck, choice, or either luck or choice? Fill in the chart. Then listen and check your work. Which of the expressions are nouns or noun phrases? Which are verb phrases? Which three were not used in the posts in exercise 1A?

be fortunate	be in the right place at the right time	chance encounter
coincidence	deliberate decision	determination
fate	life-changing experience	lucky break
(not) believe my luck	path	wind up

About luck	About choice	About luck and choice

B ▶ Now go to page 149. Do the vocabulary exercises for 9.1.

C Describe a time when you had good luck. What happened? What choices did you make in that situation?

86

3 GRAMMAR: Unreal conditionals

A   Read the sentences in the grammar box. Which rules are about the *if* clause? Which are about the result clause?

> **Unreal conditionals**
>
> **If** I **could find** her, I**'d thank** her. (I'd = I would)
>
> **If** you **hadn't met** that X-ray tech, you **might have learned** about radiology some other way.
>
> **If** my brother **hadn't broken** my finger, I **wouldn't be** an X-ray technician today.

1   Present and future unreal conditionals:

Use the past continuous, simple past, or *could* in the _____ clause.

Use *would*, *could*, or *might* + base form in the _____ clause.

2   Past unreal conditionals:

Use the past perfect in the _____ clause.

Use *would*, *could*, *may*, or *might* with *have* + past participle in the _____ clause.

3   Past unreal conditionals can also have an imaginary present result:

Use *would* + base form of a verb in the _____ clause.

B   Now go to page 137. Look at the grammar chart and do the grammar exercise for 9.1.

C   Complete the sentences and check your accuracy. Then share your ideas with a partner. Ask questions to find out more.

1   If I had more time, I _____ .

2   If I could work anywhere, I _____ .

3   I _____ if I didn't _____ .

4   If I hadn't _____ , I wouldn't _____ .

5   If I hadn't _____ , I might have _____ .

6   I couldn't have _____ if I hadn't _____ .

> ✔ **ACCURACY** CHECK
>
> In past unreal conditionals, the auxiliary *have* goes in the result clause only, not in the *if* clause.
>
> *If I hadn't ~~have~~ met the doctor, I might not have become an X-ray technician.* ✗
> *If I hadn't met the doctor, I might not have become an X-ray technician.* ✓

4 SPEAKING

A   GROUP WORK   **Think about how your life might be different now in the following situations.**

> you were born in another country   you had gone to another school
> you hadn't met someone you know   you could learn without studying
> you didn't have your present job   you had fewer/more siblings

> If I **hadn't convinced** my boss to enter the design competition, we **wouldn't have won** first prize – this amazing project that I am now leading. I'm also really **fortunate** that I have such great coworkers. I **might not enjoy** my job so much if I **weren't working** with such fantastic people.

WHY DID I DO IT?

1 LANGUAGE IN CONTEXT

A ◀» **2.19** Look at the picture. What do you think the man regrets? What other kinds of small things do people often regret? Read and listen to a group of friends talking about small regrets. How many regrets do they talk about?

◀» **2.19 Audio script**

Anne	I was just wondering what kind of things you regret doing. Not big things, like, "I wish I wasn't studying psychology. I wish I could study art instead!" Just little, silly things.
Ruby	Oh, I have a good one! Someone once told me that it's better to wash your hair with regular soap, rather than shampoo. So I tried that …
Sonia	Uh-oh, that **was a bad move**.
Ruby	I know! If only you'd been there to stop me. I couldn't get the flakes out of my hair whatever I did. And of course I had an interview to go to that day. It **was such a silly mistake**.
Sonia	That **was unfortunate**. Well, I **found myself in an awkward situation** the other day: I was on a date – a first date – and I was trying so hard to be interesting that I was talking and talking and **not watching what I was doing**. I went to take a bite of my spaghetti and spilled it all down my white top. Ordering spaghetti with tomato sauce **was such a dumb thing to do**!
David	Well, sometimes you have to **learn things the hard way**. I recently washed my new sweater in hot water, and now it's way too small. It **was completely my own fault**: The label said to use cold. **I was in too much of a hurry**, as usual. If only I had a three-year-old brother, it would fit him perfectly!
Paulo	I once ripped my pants on a dance floor!
Anne	Awkward!
Paulo	Yeah, I was on the floor, doing a breakdance move, when *rip*! But I **saw the funny side of it**. And so did everyone else!
Anne	I bet they did!
Paulo	I'**m totally incompetent at** dancing. I don't even have a sense of rhythm. I don't know what I was thinking. I could have **kicked myself**.
Anne	Well, you could have, but you might have ripped your pants even more.

B ◀» **2.19** Read and listen again. What were the friends' regrets? Who do you think made the biggest mistake?

C **PAIR WORK** **THINK CRITICALLY** Discuss the best way to deal with small regrets: laugh, forget them, try again, etc.

INSIDER ENGLISH

Use *I bet* to express agreement and show interest in what someone says.

A *I was really scared.*

B *I bet! OR I bet you were!*

A *She's so happy.*

B *I bet! OR I bet she is!*

FIND IT

2 VOCABULARY: Commenting on mistakes

A 🔊 **2.20** Look at the expressions from the text in exercise 1A on page 88 in the box. Discuss what each one means. Use a dictionary or your phone to help you. Then listen and check your work.

be a bad move	be a dumb thing to do	be a silly mistake
be incompetent (at)	be in too much of a hurry	be unfortunate
be your own fault	find yourself in an awkward situation	kick yourself
learn sth the hard way	not watch what you're doing	see the funny side of sth

B ▶ Now go to page 149. Do the vocabulary exercises for 9.2.

C PAIR WORK Describe and comment on mistakes people often make involving these things.

cleaning   clothes   computers/phones   cooking   reservations/tickets   work

3 GRAMMAR: Wishes and regrets

A Read the sentences in the grammar box. (Circle) the correct options to complete the rules.

> **Wishes and regrets**
>
> **I wish (that) I wasn't** studying psychology.   **I wish I could** study art instead.
>
> **If only you'd been** there to stop me!   **If only I had** a three-year-old brother.

1 *I wish (that)* and *if only* have **a different / the same** meaning.

2 For wishes and regrets about the present, use *I wish (that)* or *if only* followed by the simple past, **can / could**, or the past continuous.

3 For wishes and regrets about the past, use *I wish (that)* or *if only* followed by a verb in the **present perfect / past perfect**.

B ▶ Now go to page 137. Look at the grammar chart and do the grammar exercise for 9.2.

C Use *if only* to describe regrets about the problems below. Then tell a partner about similar experiences of your own using *I wish (that)*.

1 I broke it.
  If only I hadn't broken it. I wish I hadn't broken my favorite mug last week.

2 I can't find it.

3 I forgot to do it.

4 I have to go there.

5 I don't have time to do it.

6 I didn't answer it.

4 SPEAKING

A PAIR WORK Are there any little things you've done, or haven't done, in the last few days that you regret (e.g., when shopping for clothes or groceries, decorating your home, going on vacation)? For ideas, watch Carolina's video.

> Some things you **learn the hard way**. The other day I bought lots of groceries, but what I hadn't noticed was that the bag had a hole in it. **If only I'd checked** it more carefully …

EXPERT SPEAKER

Are your regrets similar to Carolina's?

MY MISTAKE

1 LISTENING

A 🔊 **2.21** **Look at the picture. What do you think the woman just did? Then listen to a call-in radio show, where she asks for advice. What did she do? How many people call in to give her advice?**

B 🔊 **2.21** **Listen again. What are the main pieces of advice the callers give to Sandy?**

C 🔊 **2.21** **IDENTIFY FEELINGS** **Listen again. Circle the word that best describes each person's feeling.**

		a		b		c	
1	Host	a	neutral	b	confused	c	annoyed
2	Marta	a	sad	b	bored	c	amused
3	Jon	a	angry	b	annoyed	c	surprised
4	Ramon	a	bored	b	sad	c	positive
5	Amanda	a	amused	b	calm	c	annoyed

D **PAIR WORK** **What advice would you give to Sandy, and why? How have you handled an awkward situation in the past?**

2 PRONUNCIATION: Listening for different word groups

A 🔊 **2.22** **Listen to how this is divided into word groups.**

Think before you write something // think again before you send it // and check who it's going to // before pushing "Send."

B 🔊 **2.23** **Listen and separate the word groups with //.**

1 Last week I wrote a personal email to a friend a very personal email but by accident I sent it to a senior manager at my company.

2 It happened to me too but with a friend not a coworker I just pretended my brother had gotten into my email and sent it as a joke.

3 That's digital communication we write and send stuff quickly and then we can't "unsend" it so we have to live with our mistakes.

C **Which statement is true about word groups?**

1 A word group has two main stresses, and there is no pause before the next word group.

2 A word group has one main stress, and it is often separated by a small pause from the next word group.

3 SPEAKING SKILLS

A 🔊 **2.21** **Match the sentence halves to make expressions of reassurance from the radio show in exercise 1A on page 90. Listen to the radio show again to check.**

Give reassurance

1	You're not the only one ___	a	it goes.
2	We all make ___	b	that bad.
3	That's the way ___	c	turn out all right.
4	What are you ___	d	who's done that.
5	It's no use ___	e	is perfect.
6	It's not ___	f	mistakes.
7	It could have ___	g	worrying about?
8	It'll ___	h	been worse.
9	No one ___	i	crying over spilled milk.

B **PAIR WORK** **THINK CRITICALLY** **Which expressions in exercise 3A are not appropriate for more formal relationships? Why? Are there any expressions in your own language like the ones in exercise 3A?**

C ▶ **Student A: Go to page 158. Student B: Go to page 159. Follow the instructions.**

4 PRONUNCIATION: Using intonation in conditional sentences

A 🔊 **2.24** **Circle the intonation pattern in this conditional sentence.**

If you'd sent the email, it could have been worse.

a If you'd sent the email ↗ // it could have been worse ↘

b If you'd sent the email ↘ // it could have been worse ↘

c If you'd sent the email ↘ // it could have been worse ↗

B 🔊 **2.25** **Underline the word group that has a falling intonation in the conditional sentences below. Listen and check, and repeat the sentences. Then finish the sentences in a different way and read them out to a partner, focusing on the intonation.**

1	If she'd listened to me	this would never have happened // we'd be in a better situation now
2	If I had thought about it more	I might have said no // I may have agreed
3	If you hadn't helped me	no one would have // I would've failed
4	If they'd told me yesterday	things might be better // I could have gotten ready

5 SPEAKING

A **PAIR WORK** **Think of a problem someone might have. Imagine you're going to talk to that person. Plan what you'll say to reassure them. Then plan how to act out your conversation.**

B **GROUP WORK** **Act out your situation for another pair. Afterward, say if you agree with the advice given. Were the expressions of reassurance appropriate?**

> I need your advice. I borrowed a suit from my friend for a party, but I lost the jacket somewhere. I don't know what to say to him – or what to do. It was an expensive suit.

> What are you worrying about? We all make mistakes. Just tell him the truth, give the pants back, and offer to help him buy a new jacket.

9.4 GOOD CONVERSATIONS

1 READING

A **PAIR WORK** **MAKE PREDICTIONS** **Read the title of the article. Why do you think the writer calls it a "happiness experiment"? Then read the article. Was your prediction correct? Was he happy at the end?**

"HOW TO MAKE SMALL TALK WITH STRANGERS:
MY 21-DAY HAPPINESS EXPERIMENT

By John Corcoran

Recently I read that people who talk to strangers are happier than those who keep quiet. I decided to test that theory with an experiment. The rules were simple: For 21 days, I would look for opportunities to talk to strangers. Here are some experiences I had.

FRIDAY, MAY 9

While visiting my hometown for a wedding, I had a chance encounter with a man in the hotel café. We started talking, and I found he had just moved there from Chicago. I told him about the community, the schools, and neighborhoods where he was thinking of buying a home.

How I Felt: The conversation made me feel useful and valuable. The man's daughter was about to enter my old high school, and he seemed relieved to hear it was a good school.

MONDAY, MAY 12

While driving home, I stopped for lunch. A man was wearing a T-shirt that said "Coastal Maine Botanical Gardens." I considered commenting on it, as we have vacationed in coastal Maine, but I didn't say anything.

How I Felt: I regret that I didn't speak up. I am curious if the gardens are close to our summer vacation spot. Sure, I can Google it, but I would have liked to chat with him about the area.

TUESDAY, MAY 20

Three men were at our house to cut our trees. I watched as they climbed the trees like monkeys and went straight to the top. I asked one of them if they fall out of trees frequently. He said, "Almost never." One said, "I've been climbing trees for 27 years," and said he fell out of a tree once and broke his knee.

How I Felt: It's not every day I talk to someone whose job is climbing trees, and it was interesting learning about how they do it.

THURSDAY, MAY 29

Today, I had to take the ferry to my office. I decided to try talking with other commuters and sat at a table. Although I exchanged a few comments, I had no meaningful conversations. At one point, I chatted with a woman, but eventually the conversation died, and she returned to reading her book.

How I Felt: I wish I'd had more conversations, but digital devices often got in the way. The important lesson I learned is to begin a conversation before people put on headphones or start reading.

FRIDAY, MAY 30

I went to a neighborhood party with my wife and our baby. The baby was a great conversation starter.

How I Felt: It's almost too easy to start talking with people when you have a baby because strangers come up and chat. I enjoyed the opportunity to meet more people.

Overall, I felt great about most of my interactions with strangers. Almost every one left me feeling a little happier. However, I will report a few disappointments: I am pretty outgoing, but I often missed an opportunity to talk because I was unsure of what to say. Second, sometimes I wanted to chat, but nearly everyone was on a digital device. I felt like speaking to them would have been interrupting. Third, I would love to report that I made new lifelong friends and found new clients. Unfortunately, that didn't happen.

MY FINAL ADVICE Just go out and try talking with strangers. It is likely that you will improve your own day and make the person you talk to happier as well.

Adapted from an article by John Corcoran on the Art of Manliness website

B **Read again. Which experiences was the writer happy about? What regrets does he have? Would you try the same experiment? Why or why not?**

C **IDENTIFY IMPLICATIONS** **Match the main things the writer learned from the experiences he had (1–5) with the correct dates (a–e).**

1 Talk about things you have in common. ____
2 Start conversations right away. ____
3 Share useful information. ____
4 Have something with you that attracts attention. ____
5 Talk to people who are different from you. ____

a Thursday, May 29
b Friday, May 30
c Friday, May 9
d Monday, May 12
e Tuesday, May 20

D **PAIR WORK** **THINK CRITICALLY** **What is "small talk"? What are good topics for "small talk" with strangers? Are there any topics it's best to avoid? Why?**

2 WRITING

A   Read the article about small talk. Summarize the tips it gives. Can you think of more tips on how to be a good listener?

SMALL TALK: HOW TO BE A GOOD LISTENER 👂

DON'T INTERRUPT

When someone else is talking, don't interrupt them. It's sometimes OK to ask a question in the middle of someone's point, for example, if you don't understand what they mean. But in general, it's best to let someone finish their point before making a comment or asking a question.

SHOW INTEREST

While you're listening to someone else, don't think about what you'll say next. Instead, show interest in their points by asking questions about the topic they're talking about. Don't change the topic or start talking about yourself.

LISTEN WITH YOUR EYES

Watch a speaker's body language, such as eye contact, hand gestures, and posture. Do they seem excited, angry, or worried? This can help you understand their feelings. Then you can ask questions, make a comment, or give advice in an appropriate way.

THINK BEFORE YOU RESPOND

Think about what you're going to say before you speak. Sometimes your opinion is helpful. Other times, it's best just to tell someone you understand or reassure them instead of telling them what you think.

REGISTER CHECK

Describe the situation using *when* or *while* before the imperative to soften the advice you give. Compare:

Strong, direct

Don't interrupt when someone else is talking.

Softer, less direct

When someone else is talking, don't interrupt them.

B   **PARALLEL STRUCTURES**   When listing items, try to use parallel structures. This means the items have the same grammatical pattern. Look at the sentences. Why are the underlined parts not parallel? Correct them with words from the article in exercise 2A.

1   **Adjectives:**   Do they seem excited, angry, or <u>are worried</u>?

2   **Noun phrases:**   Watch a speaker's body language, such as eye movement, hand gestures, and <u>how they stand.</u>

3   **Verb phrases:**   Then you can ask questions, make a comment, or <u>you should give advice</u> in an appropriate way.

✍ WRITE IT

C   **PLAN**   Think of tips for an article entitled "Small Talk: How to Be a Good Talker." Discuss the categories in the box. You can check online for more ideas. Then think about the title and structure of your article. Which tips will you include? What headings will you use for each tip? What advice/explanations will you include under each heading?

audience (who is listening)	body language (eye contact, hand gestures, posture)
content (topic)	delivery (how you speak: attitude, volume)
language (words you use)	

D   Write the article you planned. Remember to use parallel structures in lists.

E   PAIR WORK   THINK CRITICALLY   Exchange your articles. What's the best tip in your partner's article?

FIND IT

TIME TO SPEAK
Class reunion

Gaby Arnold
School of Management
BS Finance

Mark Bevilaqua
School of Nursing
BS Nursing

Mia Asner
Arts & Sciences
BA Sociology

Rodney Dacosta
Arts & Sciences
BS Mathematics

A Would you like to go to a class reunion at a school you went to years ago? How would you feel about meeting people you haven't seen for a long time? What would you talk about? Discuss with a partner.

B **PREPARE** Imagine you're going to a class reunion. Work alone to plan what you're going to talk about. Use the topics in the box. Think of important and interesting things you've done or experienced since you were a child.

education	free time	homes	regrets
relationships	sports	travel	work

C **DISCUSS** Share your news and memories with at least three people in the class and listen to what they say. As you listen, make positive comments about good things you hear and reassuring comments about not-so-good things. Encourage people to tell you more about surprising things they did.

D **PRESENT** Tell the class about the most interesting or surprising thing you heard from someone. Each time, the class asks that person to say more about it.

E **DECIDE** The class chooses the most interesting things people did or experienced.

⟫ *To check your progress, go to page 155.* ⟫

USEFUL PHRASES

DISCUSS
You were really fortunate!
It sounds like you were in the right place at the right time.
You're not the only one who …
That's the way it goes.
Was it luck or a deliberate decision?

PRESENT
You'll never guess what …
Not only that, but …
Apparently, …
Isn't that amazing?
Are you ready for this?

REVIEW 3 (UNITS 7–9)

1 VOCABULARY

A **Complete the product review with the correct forms of the expressions in the box.**

arrange	bad move	be jumbled up	be organized
be practical	be worth the money	convince	learn the hard way
purchase	regret	throw in	urge

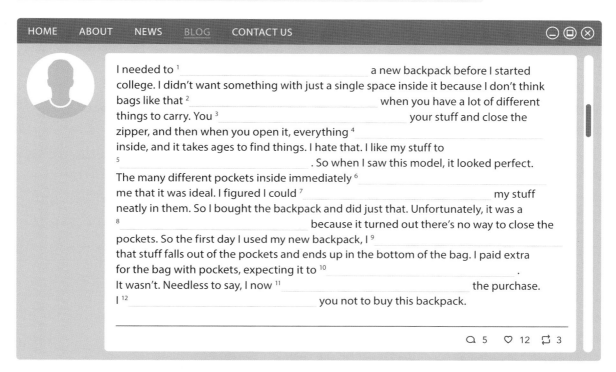

I needed to ¹ _____ a new backpack before I started college. I didn't want something with just a single space inside it because I don't think bags like that ² _____ when you have a lot of different things to carry. You ³ _____ your stuff and close the zipper, and then when you open it, everything ⁴ _____ inside, and it takes ages to find things. I hate that. I like my stuff to ⁵ _____ . So when I saw this model, it looked perfect. The many different pockets inside immediately ⁶ _____ me that it was ideal. I figured I could ⁷ _____ my stuff neatly in them. So I bought the backpack and did just that. Unfortunately, it was a ⁸ _____ because it turned out there's no way to close the pockets. So the first day I used my new backpack, I ⁹ _____ that stuff falls out of the pockets and ends up in the bottom of the bag. I paid extra for the bag with pockets, expecting it to ¹⁰ _____ . It wasn't. Needless to say, I now ¹¹ _____ the purchase. I ¹² _____ you not to buy this backpack.

⌨ 5   ♡ 12   ⇄ 3

B PAIR WORK **Tell a partner about something you bought that you were disappointed with. Use some of the phrases from exercise 1A to describe your experience.**

2 GRAMMAR

A **Use the correct forms of the verbs (*to* + verb or verb + *-ing*) in parentheses ( ) to complete the sentences.**

1 I think it's a fascinating subject _____ (read) about.

2 A lot of people don't think it's possible _____ (do) that, but I do.

3 I was dying to have something _____ (eat).

4 It's so easy to waste a lot of time _____ (do) that.

5 Because of the problem, I was forced _____ (start) the whole thing again.

6 I knew I was bound _____ (have) problems with it.

7 That's where I planned _____ (go), but in the end, it wasn't possible.

8 I get bored quickly _____ (play) that game.

9 I have trouble _____ (understand) that subject.

10 If you ask me, it's sure _____ (happen) soon.

B PAIR WORK **Think of examples of your own opinions and experiences that match the sentences in exercise 2A. Tell a partner about them.**

VOCABULARY

A **Complete the sentences with the words in the box.**

> break   difference   ease   encounter   expected
> lesson   life   life-changing pleasure   time

1 To be successful, you need a lucky _____ .
2 Generally speaking, if you take _____ in doing something, you'll do it well.
3 Mistakes are the best way to learn because they always teach you a(n) _____ you won't forget.
4 It's often the small things, not the big things, that make a(n) _____ .
5 If you want to learn a new skill, you should do it on your own _____ .
6 You can expect to change careers at some point – not to devote your _____ to one occupation.
7 Planning things in detail isn't very helpful, since things hardly ever go as _____ .
8 If someone is doing something with _____ , it usually means they're good at it.
9 Learning to speak a second language is a(n) _____ experience for several reasons.
10 The best way to meet your future husband or wife is through a chance _____ .

B   PAIR WORK **Say whether you agree, partly agree, or disagree with the sentences in exercise 3A. Say why and give examples to help explain your views.**

4 GRAMMAR

A Circle **the correct options.**
1 One day, I'm *learning / going to learn* to ride a motorcycle.
2 I'm sure next week *might be / will be* fairly relaxing.
3 According to my schedule, *I'm having / I'd have* my next English lesson tomorrow.
4 Tonight, I *might / would* do some work at home or maybe just get some rest.
5 This time next year, *I'll study / I'll be studying* in college.
6 If I *moved / would move* to Europe, I would live in Spain.
7 If I *could / would* have a free plane ticket to anywhere in the world, I'd go to South Korea.
8 Out of all foreign languages, I wish I *can / could* speak Korean.

B   PAIR WORK **Say which sentences from exercise 4A are true for you, or change them so they are true for you.**

WEST

SAN BERNARDINO
66
COUNTY

UNIT OBJECTIVES

- talk about people's characteristics
- talk about customer research
- give your impressions
- write a professional profile
- develop a plan to improve a company website

PEOPLE, PROFILES

10

START SPEAKING

A   When you look at the picture, what do you think of the person? Would it be a good choice for a profile picture? What kind of profile would it be appropriate for?

B   Talk about a profile picture you have for social media, work/college, or on an ID card. What impression does it give about the kind of person you are? Is it a true impression?

C   What kind of things do people change about their appearance when they want to make a specific impression in these situations: an extended family gathering, going on a date, a job interview, making new friends? For ideas, watch Lucia's video.

EXPERT SPEAKER

Do you agree with Lucia? Can you think of more examples?

ARE WE UNIQUE?

1 LANGUAGE IN CONTEXT

A   PAIR WORK   Look at the picture. How do you think the people are connected?

B   Read the article. How did the author try to find her doppelgänger? Would you want to meet your doppelgänger?

Doppelgängers are people who look alike but aren't related to each other.

⊗ ▣ ⊖

| Home | About | Blog | Contact Us |

Maxine Frith

Can you find your doppelgänger in a day?
by Maxine Frith

Doppelgänger means "double walker," that is, someone walking around this planet that looks just like you. It is said that we are each likely to have at least seven **look-alikes** somewhere in the world. I wondered about the possibility of discovering a few of mine.

I posted a message and picture on Facebook, Twitter, and Instagram, but it didn't result in finding anyone with my **likeness**. Next, I used the "I Look Like You" website, which uses facial recognition software to compare your image with millions of others. The site matched me with a **female** named Kathryn Laskaris. She wasn't a perfect **match**, but we have a similar **look**.

Next, I tried some doppelgänger-matching apps. I was matched with a 20-something **male** and a

baby. Finally, I uploaded my photo into a Google Images search and then clicked to search for something "visually similar." Within seconds, my doppelgänger appeared: Michal Ben-Josef Hirsch. I stared at her, noticing our **similarities** – she has the same **features** as me, the same hair, and the same smile. She's also smart and successful – everything I could hope for in a twin stranger.

I was really interested in learning more. Psychologist Amima Memon explains, "It may seem bizarre that people become obsessed with finding strangers who look exactly like them, but … research shows that … we like people who look like us … ."

I haven't succeeded in learning more about Michal. I suppose I'll just have to be happy with me.

Adapted from an article by Maxine Frith in The Telegraph

C   Read the article again. What matches did the author get? How were they similar to her?

D   GROUP WORK   THINK CRITICALLY   How would you feel about your doppelgänger contacting you?

2 VOCABULARY: Describing characteristics

FIND IT

A   🔊 2.26   What do the nouns in the box mean? Use a dictionary or your phone to help you. Then listen and check. Can you remember which eight were used in the text? Which three words can also be adjectives?

| build | characteristic | feature | female | gender | individual |
| likeness | look | look-alike | male | match | similarity |

B   ▶ Now go to page 150. Do the vocabulary exercises for 10.1.

C   PAIR WORK   Describe yourself and some of your typical characteristics using the words in exercise 2A.

3 GRAMMAR: Gerunds after prepositions

A Read the sentences in the grammar box. Circle the correct options to complete the rules.

> **Gerunds after prepositions**
>
> I wondered about **the possibility of discovering** a few of mine.
> I **was** really **interested in learning** more.
> I haven't **succeeded in learning** more about Michal.

1 You can use a gerund (verb + -ing) **before** / **after** some phrases with a noun + of.
2 You can use the verb **be** / **have** + an adjective + a preposition + a gerund.
3 You can use a gerund as **an object** / **a subject** after a verb + preposition.

B ▶ Now go to page 138. Look at the grammar chart and do the grammar exercise for 10.1.

C PAIR WORK What are different ways of meeting new people?
Make questions with a gerund and your own ideas. Use the
prompts below to help you. Check your accuracy. Then ask another
pair the questions.

1 places for / ways of meeting new people
   Have you ever thought of meeting people online?
2 things you would most care about / be interested in
3 things you could plan on doing
4 things you might be concerned about / risks

✓ **ACCURACY** CHECK

Be sure to use the correct form after
a verb + preposition.
*It didn't result in ~~find~~ anyone with my
likeness.* ✗
*It didn't result in ~~to find~~ anyone with my
likeness.* ✗
*It didn't result in finding anyone with
my likeness.* ✓

4 SPEAKING

A GROUP WORK Do you like to be similar to your friends or different? Discuss using the topics below and your
own ideas. Do most people in your group like to be similar or different?

clothes	education	experiences	goals	hairstyle
hobbies/interests	humor	music	personality	

I often wear trendy clothes. I like the **idea of
looking** like my favorite celebrities.

I **wouldn't dream of dressing** like other people.
I like to be an **individual** and have my own **look**.

1   LANGUAGE IN CONTEXT

A 🔊 **2.27** **What kinds of information do you think companies collect about their customers, and why? Discuss with a partner. Then read and listen to a radio interview with Lina, a marketing executive. Were your ideas correct?**

🔊 **2.27 Audio script**

Host   We all know that companies collect a lot of information about us as customers. Why do they do it?

Lina   Well, basically it allows them to **identify** your needs and understand what kinds of things you might want to buy.

Host   So, what kind of information do they collect?

Lina   Well, it can be things like gender, family situation, age, profession, um … financial situation, interests. It could also include likes, goals, … fears. This is the kind of information companies can get from social media, **surveys**, and from past purchases you made.

Host   OK. And how is this information used?

Lina   Well, let's say a store is **analyzing** a list of customers' purchases for a month. This list lets the store **calculate** how much the customer spent. And the store can also **examine** the types of purchases to see what they reveal. So let's say this person spent $280 on lipstick, expensive sunglasses, baby clothes, two different products to prevent insects from biting, a video game, two tablet cases, and three books: about leadership, negotiating, and Italian cooking. Now, what does an **analysis** of that information **demonstrate**? It allows the store to figure out a lot about this person and helps the store *guess* other things. And that **assessment** enables the store to predict how much this person might spend per month and what other products they might want to buy.

B 🔊 **2.27** **Read and listen again. How do companies get information about their customers? Why is it useful?**

C **PAIR WORK** **How do you feel about companies collecting different kinds of information about you? For ideas, watch Lucia's video.**

EXPERT SPEAKER

Do you agree with Lucia? How, do you think, does Lucia's job inform her answer?

2   VOCABULARY: Describing research

FIND IT

A 🔊 **2.28** **PAIR WORK** **Look at the words in the box. Discuss their meanings. Use a dictionary or your phone to help you. Which are verbs? Nouns? Then listen and check the parts of speech. Were verbs or nouns used out of each pair in the interview in exercise 1A?**

analyze/analysis	assess/assessment	calculate/calculation	demonstrate/demonstration
examine/examination	identify/identification	survey/survey	

B ▶ **Now go to page 150. Do the vocabulary exercises for 10.2.**

C **PAIR WORK** **THINK CRITICALLY** **Look again at the customer's purchases in exercise 1A. What can you figure out, or guess, about this person? Think about: family situation, age, profession, financial situation, interests, likes, goals, and fears. Then compare your ideas with others in the class.**

> We can **identify** the person's interests. They bought lipstick and expensive sunglasses so that **demonstrates** that they care about their appearance.

3 GRAMMAR: Causative verbs

A **Read the sentences in the grammar box. Complete the rules with the options in the box. There is one option you do not need to use. Which verbs do we use to talk about things we do <u>not</u> want to happen?**

> **Causative verbs**
>
> It **allows them to identify** your needs.
>
> … two different products to **prevent insects from biting** …
>
> | base form of the verb | gerund | infinitive |

> **!** We use *let, make,* and *have +* base form of the verb when something or someone causes something to happen.
>
> *This list **lets** the store calculate how much the customer spent.*

1 After *allow, cause, enable*: Use an object + _____ .

2 After *keep, prevent, protect, stop*: Use an object + *from* + _____ .

B ▶ **Now go to page 138. Look at the grammar chart and do the grammar exercise for 10.2.**

C **Complete the sentences about shopping habits with your own ideas. Then compare with a partner. Ask questions to find out more.**

1 Shopping for new things makes me _____ .

2 Having a mall nearby helps me _____ .

3 Credit cards allow me _____ .

4 Nothing can stop me _____ .

5 Online shopping enables me _____ .

6 Having a budget prevents me _____ .

4 SPEAKING

A **A new department store is opening near you. Write down some customer information about yourself. Explain what you want and need there. Use these headings:**

1 Description (of me)   2 What I want/need to buy   3 What facilities I want/need to use

List three to five things under each heading.

B [PAIR WORK] **Analyze your partner's profile. Then give your assessment of products and services that would be of interest to your partner. Say why.**

> I've **examined** your profile and found you like eating out with friends. If the store had a restaurant, that would **allow you and your friends to eat** there.

> I like that idea. And I've **identified** you as someone interested in fashion. **To help you** find what you want, the store definitely needs to offer a variety of clothing styles.

A CAREFUL CHOICE

1 LISTENING

A   **PAIR WORK**   Imagine you need to order a cake for a party. What kind of things would you need to consider to make a good choice?

B   🔊 **2.29** Listen to two friends deciding which company to order a cake from. Why do they want a cake? How many companies do they consider? How do they feel at the end?

C   🔊 **2.29** **LISTEN FOR CONTRASTING IDEAS** Listen again. List the strong points and weak points of each cake company and its products. Then predict which cake company you think they'll choose. Which one would you choose?

D   🔊 **2.30** Listen to the rest of the conversation. Which cake company did they choose, and why?

E   **PAIR WORK**   **THINK CRITICALLY** How can you tell if a company and its products are good when you're shopping online? For example, what can web design, photos, reviews, and the range of products for sale reveal?

2 PRONUNCIATION: Quoting from a text

A   🔊 **2.31** Listen to the speaker reading aloud from the cake website. Which parts are direct quotations? Add quotation marks " " around these parts. How are these pronounced differently?

The company profile says cakes for all occasions, designs for all themes and budgets, and skilled, professional cake decorating. That all sounds good.

It also says free personal advice – that's nice.

B   🔊 **2.32** Look at the quoted section in the extract below. How would this be pronounced differently? Listen and check.

Madrona Cakes … "freshly baked, a variety of flavors, reasonable prices." And they also make cakes low in sugar, cakes with no egg, and dairy-free cakes.

C   **PAIR WORK**   Look back at the article on page 98. Choose a short extract to quote to your partner, like in exercises A and B above. Prepare your whole sentence (including the direct quotation from the article). Then say it to your partner. Can your partner identify which words came directly from the text?

FIND IT

3 SPEAKING SKILLS

A PAIR WORK Look at the expressions from the conversation in exercises 1B and 1C on page 102. Discuss the meaning of the underlined words. Use a dictionary or your phone to help you.

Give your impressions

1 I have a <u>funny feeling</u> (that) …
2 I get the <u>impression</u> (that) …
3 <u>From what I can see</u>, …
4 I have a <u>hunch</u> (that) …
5 <u>Judging by</u> the description, …
6 My <u>gut feeling</u> is (that) …
7 <u>What strikes me</u> (about …) is (that) …
8 <u>As far as I can tell</u>, …

B PAIR WORK Imagine you are in the following situations. Give your impressions.

1 You are standing in front of a new restaurant. You can see inside, and you can see the menu on the window. One of you thinks it looks good (clean, comfortable, good food). The other does not (crowded, noisy, not enough food choices).

Hmm, from what I can see, this restaurant looks …

> **INSIDER** ENGLISH
>
> *lose track of time* = forget when something is due or supposed to happen, often because of being busy with other things

2 You have to turn in a research and writing assignment on ancient pyramids. You lost track of time, and it's due tomorrow. One of you thinks you can finish in time (easy to find information, can divide the work, can stay up late). The other does not (takes time to research, no time to work together, have other homework).

About our essay, I have a funny feeling that I won't be able to … because …

4 PRONUNCIATION: Recognizing /eɪ/, /aɪ/, /ɔɪ/

A 🔊 2.33 <u>Underline</u> the /eɪ/, /aɪ/, and /ɔɪ/ sounds. Listen and check your work. Then repeat.

1 What strikes me about this place is the choice of cakes.
2 I have a funny feeling that I may enjoy it.
3 Try one of our nice and tasty pies – you won't be disappointed!

B 🔊 2.34 Circle the word that has a different diphthong.

1	straight	climb	fail
2	voice	joy	ache
3	weight	cycle	height

4	break	crayon	finally
5	design	choice	voyage

C PAIR WORK Write down six of the words from exercise 4B. Take turns reading aloud one of the words from exercise 4B, saying the diphthong carefully. If you hear the word on your list from your partner, cross it out. The first student to cross out six words is the winner.

5 SPEAKING

A PAIR WORK You want to join a gym. Look at the online profiles of three gyms on page 158. Discuss the gyms, giving your impressions of each. Decide which one you'd each like to join and why. Then check with another pair and see if they had similar impressions and chose the same ones.

*Well, **judging by** the description, gym 3 is modern and pretty large.*

*I agree, and **as far as I can tell**, it has good facilities. For example, …*

A PROFESSIONAL PROFILE

1 READING

A **Is it a good idea to have a profile on a social networking site for professionals? Why or why not? Read the article. Why does the author have a profile? Why does she decide she needs to improve it?**

I recently graduated from college and am looking for a job. I joined a social network for professionals and wrote a fantastic profile for my page. I was sure that the first employer who read it would want to hire me.

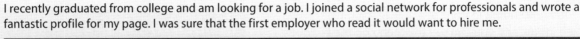

KINSLEY GORDON

last updated six months ago

Contact me at 646-555-4302 or by email.

I am an individual with a unique personality, and I work very well with others. I recently graduated from New York University from the Gallatin School of Individualized Study. I put together my own program combining several areas of study. I hope to work for an English–Japanese bilingual company in the marketing department. In college, I had an internship at VTL-Wire, a large tech company. I also wrote poetry for a community magazine. Right now, I'm doing part-time freelance work, but I want to work full-time. Please contact me to find out how my skills could best work for your company.

No employers were responding, so I started reading articles about how to write a good profile. Mack Gelber, in his article called "8 Ways to Make Your Social Media Profile an Employer Magnet," had some really good advice. Here are some of his main points:

1 Have a complete and relevant profile

Make sure your profile contains your complete employment history and education, as well as any skills related to your job. Try to think through the eyes of an employer – no one wants to see a half-written profile.

2 Highlight skills and achievements that help employers

In your career history, be careful about the information you include. We don't need to know about how you organized the office softball team. Instead, try talking about specific goals you've met, and support your information with numbers. For example: "Sold $X while cutting costs by Y%."

3 Update your profile frequently

It's important to stay active on all social media sites. Start a new job? Post an update. Get a promotion? Update your title.

4 Keep your connections career-focused

Getting requests to connect from old roommates and people you don't remember from high school is only to be expected on social media, but you want to make sure the majority of the people you're connected to have similar career goals. This gives employers the impression that you're serious about your career.

5 Provide a clear link to your email address

Say an employer sees your profile and wants to get in touch with you about a potential job opportunity. Can they find your email address in a few seconds? Make sure it's linked somewhere that's clear and easy to see.

6 Have a professional-looking headshot

A good headshot is key to having a strong profile. That's not to say you need to wear formal office clothing (business casual is fine), but it pays to look engaged and put together.

Adapted from an article by Mack Gelber on the Monster website

B **TAKE NOTES** **Read again. Take notes about each of the six points. Summarize each one with a phrase or two. Then share your notes with a partner. Were your ideas the same?**

C **THINK CRITICALLY** **According to Gelber's points, what problems does Kinsley's profile have? What do you think she could do to improve it?**

2 WRITING

A **THINK CRITICALLY** Read Kinsley's new profile. What improvements did she make from her profile in exercise 1A on page 104?

KINSLEY GORDON
last updated yesterday

Marketing and more

I'm a recent graduate of New York University from the Gallatin School of Individualized Study who is dedicated to doing my best. I work very well on my own and with others. In order to focus on a marketing career, my field of study combined business, Japanese, and creative writing. I hope to work for an English–Japanese bilingual company in the marketing department. In college, I had an internship at VTL-Wire, a large tech company. My responsibilities included making online product demonstrations in English and Japanese, analyzing the comments people made on the demonstrations, and reporting people's impressions of the products to the company. I'm tech-savvy and learn new programs quickly. Although I'm currently doing part-time freelance work helping people design their websites, my ultimate goal is to work for a company full-time. I realize the benefits of starting small, especially at a company where there's the possibility of career progression. Please contact me to find out how my skills could best work for your company.

646-555-4302 • www.kinsleysays.com • kgordon@mailme.net • CONNECTIONS 225

REGISTER CHECK

Contractions are not normally used in formal writing. However, it's OK to use contractions on social media, like professional job sites.

Résumé, cover letter, etc.
I am tech-savvy and learn new programs quickly.

Social media site/profile
I'm tech-savvy and learn new programs quickly.

GLOSSARY

progression (*n*) when someone goes up to the next level or stage

B **USE PROFESSIONAL LANGUAGE** Read about three things to avoid when using professional language. Look at the examples, and then find good versions of each in Kinsley's profile in exercise 2A.

1 Don't use slang (= very informal language).

not: I'm uber-excited to work for a company 24/7.

2 Avoid words like *kind of*, *probably*, and *maybe*. Use language that makes you sound confident.

not: I'm kind of tech-savvy and probably can learn new programs pretty fast.

3 Don't be negative. Be positive and polite.

not: I'm not sure I have the experience you're looking for, but contact me to see if my skills might work for your company.

 **WRITE IT**

C **PLAN** You're going to create a professional profile on a social networking site. Tell your partner about the education, skills, and characteristics you have that make you a good candidate for future jobs. Then look at the profile in exercise 2A. What kind of information do you need to include at the beginning and end? How long should your profile be?

D Write your professional profile. Be sure to use professional language.

E **PAIR WORK** Exchange profiles. Does your partner use professional language? Can you suggest any improvements?

10.5

TIME TO SPEAK
Attracting talent

LESSON OBJECTIVE
- develop a plan to improve a company website

Tech company

Hospital

Restaurant

Engineering company

A   **PREPARE**   In pairs, imagine you are experts who give advice to companies on how to make the career section of their website as attractive as possible to first-time employees. Choose a type of company from the pictures above or use your own idea.

B   **DISCUSS**   In pairs, brainstorm answers to this question: What do most first-time employees think about when choosing a company to work for? For example:

career progression   kinds of jobs available   products the company makes
training opportunities   workplace environment

C   Compare your ideas with other pairs. Which areas do people think are most important?

D   **DECIDE**   In your original pairs, consider all the ideas you have. Decide which three areas are the most important to first-time employees of the company you chose in part A. Then decide how to present these areas on the company website in order to attract these employees. Use some of these options and your own ideas: photos, videos, interviews, reviews.

E   **PRESENT**   Tell the class what type of company you chose, present your ideas, and explain why first-time employees will like them.

F   **AGREE**   After the presentations, decide as a class which ideas will be most attractive to first-time employees. Then discuss which company you would like to work for.

To check your progress, go to page 156.

USEFUL PHRASES

DISCUSS
I get the impression that …
Judging by the people I know, …
Judging by what I've heard, …
As far as I can tell, …
My assessment is (that) …

PRESENT
This will allow first-time employees to …
This will help them …
This will enable them to …

UNIT OBJECTIVES

- talk about fake goods
- talk about untrue information
- express belief and disbelief
- write a persuasive essay
- share tips on solutions

REALLY?

11

START SPEAKING

A   Do you think this picture is real or fake? Why do you think so?

B   Can you think of some examples of fake photos you've seen? How easy or difficult is it to see that the photos are fakes?

C   When and why do some people choose to edit their photos? List the reasons. What kind of changes might they make to their photos? How do you feel about this? Answer the questions. For ideas, watch Bojan's video.

EXPERT SPEAKER

Do you agree with Bojan's opinion? Can you think of any other examples?

FAKE!

1 LANGUAGE IN CONTEXT

A **Look at the picture of fake goods being destroyed. Do you think it's a waste? Read the newspaper article. What fake goods does the journalist mention?**

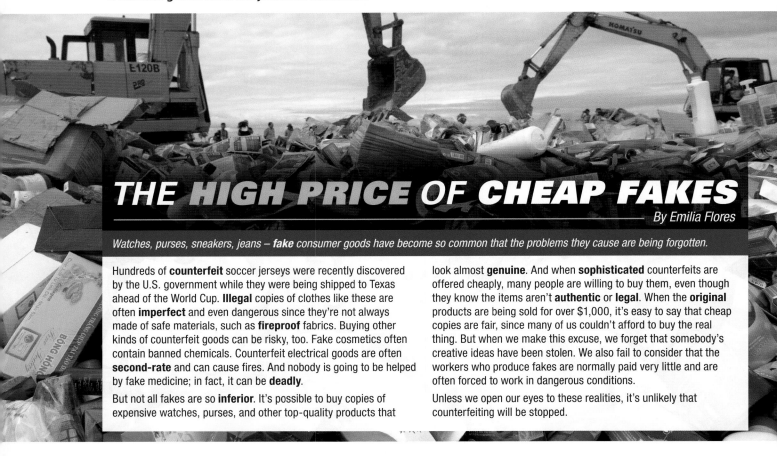

THE HIGH PRICE OF CHEAP FAKES
By Emilia Flores

*Watches, purses, sneakers, jeans – **fake** consumer goods have become so common that the problems they cause are being forgotten.*

Hundreds of **counterfeit** soccer jerseys were recently discovered by the U.S. government while they were being shipped to Texas ahead of the World Cup. **Illegal** copies of clothes like these are often **imperfect** and even dangerous since they're not always made of safe materials, such as **fireproof** fabrics. Buying other kinds of counterfeit goods can be risky, too. Fake cosmetics often contain banned chemicals. Counterfeit electrical goods are often **second-rate** and can cause fires. And nobody is going to be helped by fake medicine; in fact, it can be **deadly**.

But not all fakes are so **inferior**. It's possible to buy copies of expensive watches, purses, and other top-quality products that look almost **genuine**. And when **sophisticated** counterfeits are offered cheaply, many people are willing to buy them, even though they know the items aren't **authentic** or **legal**. When the **original** products are being sold for over $1,000, it's easy to say that cheap copies are fair, since many of us couldn't afford to buy the real thing. But when we make this excuse, we forget that somebody's creative ideas have been stolen. We also fail to consider that the workers who produce fakes are normally paid very little and are often forced to work in dangerous conditions.

Unless we open our eyes to these realities, it's unlikely that counterfeiting will be stopped.

B **Read the article again. According to the journalist, what problems do fake goods cause?**

C PAIR WORK THINK CRITICALLY **Which do you think is the most serious of these problems? Why? To what extent do you agree with the journalist's opinion?**

2 VOCABULARY: Describing consumer goods

FIND IT

A ◀)) **2.35** PAIR WORK **Look at the words from the article in exercise 1A in the box. Discuss their meaning. Use a dictionary or your phone to help you. Then listen and check your work.**

authentic	counterfeit	deadly	fake	fireproof
genuine	illegal	imperfect	inferior	legal
original	second-rate	sophisticated		

B ▶ **Now go to page 151. Do the vocabulary exercises for 11.1.**

C PAIR WORK **Have you ever seen or bought fake goods? What were they like? How can customers tell the difference between counterfeit and authentic goods?**

3 GRAMMAR: Passive forms

A **Read the sentences in the grammar box. Circle the correct options to complete the rules. Then add the correct passive form (a–f) to complete the rules (3–8).**

> ### Passive forms
>
> Counterfeit soccer jerseys **were** recently **discovered** by the U.S. government while they **were being shipped** to Texas.
>
> They**'re** not always **made** of safe materials.
>
> Nobody **is going to be helped** by fake medicine. It's unlikely that counterfeiting **will be stopped**.
>
> The original products **are being sold** for over $1,000.
>
> We forget that somebody's creative ideas **have been stolen**.

We use passive forms when we don't know, or it's not important, who [1]**did / received** the action. The person or thing [2]**doing / receiving** the action is more important, so it becomes the subject of the sentence.

a	simple past	**3**	The ___ passive: *am/is/are* + past participle.
b	past continuous	**4**	The ___ passive: *was/were* + past participle.
c	simple present	**5**	The ___ passive: *has/have been* + past participle.
d	future	**6**	The ___ passive: *will + be* + past participle <u>or</u> *am/is/are going to + be* + past participle.
e	present continuous	**7**	The ___ passive: *am/is/are + being* + past participle.
f	present perfect	**8**	The ___ passive: *was/were + being* + past participle.

B ▶ **Now go to page 138. Look at the grammar chart and do the grammar exercise for 11.1.**

C PAIR WORK **Make sentences about counterfeit goods using these words, passive forms, and your own ideas. Check your accuracy. Then compare with another pair.**

1 Fake sunglasses / sell / in my city

2 In the future, / fake products / sell

3 Not long ago, / buy / by teenagers

4 Discover / by the police / recently

> ✔ **ACCURACY** CHECK
>
> **Don't forget to use the auxiliary *be* in continuous tenses: correct form of *be* + *being* + past participle.**
>
> *Counterfeit soccer jerseys were discovered while they* ~~were shipping~~ *to Texas.* ✗
> *Counterfeit soccer jerseys were discovered while they were being shipped to Texas.* ✓

4 SPEAKING

A GROUP WORK **Where are counterfeit goods usually sold? Why do people buy them? Discuss using the ideas below. Then compare your answers with the class.**

Fake goods: accessories, clothes, cosmetics, electronic goods, shoes, etc.

Illegal copies: books, computer games, DVDs/Blu-rays, music, software, etc.

> Fake brand-name watches **have been sold** in our city's markets for years. These days, they**'re** sometimes **found** in stores, too. They're usually second-rate, but people buy them because …

INTERNET TALES

FIND IT

1 VOCABULARY: Degrees of truth

A 🔊 **2.36** **PAIR WORK** **Look at the words in the box. Describe them in other words. Use a dictionary or your phone to help you. Which are adjectives? Nouns or noun phrases? Then listen and check the parts of speech.**

accurate	biased	controversial	dishonest	exaggerated
false	hoax	inaccurate	misinformation	misleading
rumor	suspicious	trustworthy	urban legend	white lie

B ➤ **Now go to page 151. Do the vocabulary exercises for 11.2.**

2 LANGUAGE IN CONTEXT

A 🔊 **2.37** **Read and listen to a radio show about five possibly fake stories. What are they about? Then answer the host's last question with a partner.**

🔊 2.37 Audio script

Host Today's topic is **rumors**, **urban legends**, and other fake stuff on the internet. When I was ten, I told my parents the moon landing was filmed in a TV studio. They said that was a lie, but I replied, "No, it's true. I read it on the internet!" I didn't expect to be laughed at, but I was. I learned, as we all do, that you can't always trust the web. So, I asked my listeners for internet stories that might be **false**. Listen to a few. Here's Raúl from Doral, Florida.

Raúl I read that hundreds of deadly snakes escaped from a truck that crashed in our town. But I never heard anything more, so I guess the information was **exaggerated** or **inaccurate**. This kind of **misinformation** has to be stopped because in the end, all news becomes **suspicious**.

Host Nina from Denver, Colorado, said this.

Nina Recently I saw a photo of a purple watermelon on Snapchat. It was probably a **hoax**. People say **misleading** photos shouldn't be posted, but they usually don't do any harm.

Host Let's listen to Gabe from Portland, Oregon.

Gabe I read online that there are more trees on Earth than stars in the galaxy. That can't be **accurate**! All online articles need to be checked. But where do you check? Online?

Host And Britt called in, all the way from Windsor in Canada.

Britt A video of a human-looking robot walking down a street went viral. A few people thought robots were taking over the world! If you look closely, the video seems to be made on a computer. I don't think it's from a **trustworthy** site.

Host So, are these stories true or not? I'll tell you after the break.

GLOSSARY
the galaxy (*n*) a very large group of stars that contains our sun and the planets that go around it

B 🔊 **2.37** **Read and listen again. Which speakers explain why they think the information is false? What are their reasons?**

C 🔊 **2.38** **Listen to the end of the program. Were the stories true or not?**

D **GROUP WORK** **THINK CRITICALLY** **Do you think the internet spreads more truth or lies? Why? For ideas, watch Bojan's video. Can you think of some recent examples?**

EXPERT SPEAKER

Do you agree with Bojan? What do you think of his solution?

3 GRAMMAR: Passives with modals and modal-like expressions; passive infinitives

A Read the sentences in the grammar box. Complete the rules about the passive with *be* or *to be*.

Passives with modals and modal-like expressions	Passive infinitives
Misleading photos **shouldn't be posted**. This kind of misinformation **has to be stopped**. All online articles **need to be checked**.	I **didn't expect to be laughed at**. The video **seems to be made** on a computer.

1 After modals, like *should* and *could*, use _____ + a past participle.

2 After modal-like expressions, like *have to*, *need to*, and *had better*, use _____ + a past participle.

3 After verbs like *expect*, *seem*, and *want*, use _____ + a past participle.

> **!** In the passive, the main verb is always in its past participle form, never the base form. So, for passives after modals and modal-like expressions, use *be* + past participle, not the base form. Something **has to be done** to stop fake stories from spreading.

B ▶ Now go to page 139. Look at the grammar chart and do the grammar exercise for 11.2.

C Complete the sentences with the correct passive form of the verbs in parentheses ( ) and your own ideas. Then compare with a partner. Do you agree with your partner's ideas?

1 If we ... , we are _____ (not be likely / believe) by anyone.

2 I think controversial issues _____ (shouldn't / discuss) during ...

3 Friends _____ (must / inform) when our social media photos are ...

4 I _____ (hope / tell) the truth when I ...

5 We _____ (could / trick) by reading ... , so be careful.

6 I only _____ (want / tell) white lies if ...

4 SPEAKING

FIND IT

A [PAIR WORK] **What stories have you heard or read online that weren't true? You can look online for stories if you want. Did people believe them? Why? Did you believe them at first?**

> I read that alligators live in the sewers in New York City. I think people believed the story because it gave a lot of **accurate** information about alligators. But the article had a lot of grammar mistakes and **seemed to be written** by a teenager, so I thought it was a **hoax** right away.

B [GROUP WORK] **Share two of your stories with another pair. Do you think stories like this need to be stopped? Why or why not?**

> **Urban legends**, like alligators in the sewers, **shouldn't be spread** because they make people panic.

11.3 BELIEVE IT OR NOT …

1 LISTENING

A   Do you often look at the night sky? What kind of things do you think of? What questions would you ask someone who's been in space?

B   ◀)) 2.39 Listen to Damon and his friends talking about the NASA Parker Solar Probe. How many of them definitely believe the probe is going to the sun?

C   ◀)) 2.39 UNDERSTAND IMPORTANT DETAILS Listen again. What arguments do the friends make for and against the story?

D   ◀)) 2.40 Listen to part of a news program about the Parker Solar Probe. What's the significance of these numbers?

   a   6 million   b   several million   c   1,400

E   THINK CRITICALLY Who is more believable, Damon or Rose? Why? How can you normally tell if someone is telling the truth?

2 PRONUNCIATION: Listening for intonation on exclamations and imperatives

A   ◀)) 2.41 Listen to the high falling intonation on exclamations and imperatives.

   Yeah, right, Damon! ⟶   Tell me another one! ⟶

B   ◀)) 2.42 Listen and mark the high falling intonation.

   1   The connection's worse than in outer space!   4   Wow! That's hot!
   2   They're going to land at night!   5   That's still hot!
   3   I'm telling you, it's true!

C   Circle the correct option to complete the sentence.

   There is a *high/low / fall/rise* intonation on exclamations and imperatives.

3 SPEAKING SKILLS

A Match the correct headings from the box to each column. Write headings in the correct places. Would high falling intonation occur in any of these expressions? If so, where?

> Belief   Disbelief   Some belief

Yeah, right! Tell me another one. I find that hard to believe. There's no truth in it/that.	Maybe there's some truth in it. It's/That's partly true.	… , believe it or not. I'm absolutely positive (that) …

B `PAIR WORK` Take turns saying these rumors and expressing belief or disbelief about them.

1 By 2025, we'll be able to text just by thinking.
2 It won't be long before people will be settled on the moon.
3 In the next 20 years, there will be no ice in the Arctic.
4 Dinosaurs have been created in a lab somewhere, using DNA from fossils.
5 The number of people who own cars will soon decline, and car-sharing will be used instead.
6 Young people will increasingly work online from home, so they'll be able to live anywhere.

4 PRONUNCIATION: Saying /oʊ/ and /aʊ/

A ◀) **2.43** Listen to the difference between the /oʊ/ and /aʊ/ sounds.

/oʊ/	/aʊ/		/oʊ/	/aʊ/
no	now		tone	town
coach	couch		load	loud
known	noun			

B ◀) **2.44** Choose a suitable word with either an /oʊ/ or /aʊ/ sound to put in the conversation. Then listen to check your work.

A I don't believe a p_____ could g_____ s_____ far into space. H_____ a_____ you?

B It'd be difficult, but it's possible, th_____. Maybe not n_____ but in ten years or s_____.

A Come on, there's z_____ chance! I d_____ k_____ much a_____ science, but that's impossible.

B There's n_____ reason why not. When it happens, I'll say, "I t_____ you s_____!"

C `PAIR WORK` Read the conversation aloud, focusing on the /oʊ/ and /aʊ/ sounds.

5 SPEAKING

A `PAIR WORK` Create a role play of two people discussing a rumor, real or imaginary, about one of the topics in the box. Express belief or disbelief about the rumor. Practice your role play and then act it out for another pair. They express belief or disbelief about the rumor, as well.

> college/workplace   food/health   places in your city or country
> politics   sports/entertainment

I heard a **rumor** that final exams **are going to be canceled** and that students **will** only **be graded** on their coursework.

Yeah, I heard that, too, but **there's no truth in it**. It was a **false** story started by some students who wish it was true!

CONVINCE ME

1 READING

A | SUMMARIZE KEY POINTS | Have you ever trusted a review that turned out to be fake? Read the article. Why do companies want to stop fake reviews? What can we do to figure out if reviews are fake? Summarize each of the nine tips.

SPOT 'EM –

Fake product reviews

by Ken Evoy

Companies depend on hundreds of thousands of consumer reviews that point you to "the best of whatever." They work hard to minimize fake reviews because it's good business to prevent customer disappointment due to inaccurate information. There are honest reviews, of course, but you still need to check reviews yourself, whether you're buying a book, a hotel room, or a Ferrari. Here are some tips to help you.

1 Fight technology with technology

A good way to assess whether a review is computer-generated is to use a computer program. *Fakespot* is an online tool that helps you figure out which reviews are trustworthy and which are not. Simply paste a review's URL into Fakespot's search engine to get results. It may not always be totally accurate, but it's a good place to start.

2 Check the reviewer's profile

Most sites ask users to register before leaving a review. Click on the username to see past reviews. Most "real" people buy a wide range of products from large companies, so they'll have a wide range of reviews.

3 Compensation

Is this review paid? Did the reviewer receive the product in return for a review? If so, it's not necessarily fake – but it may be biased.

4 Review quality

Reviews that rely on individuals being paid small amounts of money to write as many as possible will be short and nonspecific. The goal is to put the item into the five-star category quickly by posting as many "excellent" reviews as possible. So the author needs to be able to copy and paste a large number in a short time. Look for phrases like "great product" or "wonderful service."

5 Lack of detail

Researchers found that some reviewers of hotel rooms did not talk about the specifics of the hotel at all. They couldn't – they had never been there. So they'd write instead about the *reason* they were there. "Spent a wonderful weekend here with the family" and "will always use this hotel for future business trips" are the kinds of things that show a hotel review might be fake.

6 Lack of experience

Similarly, if the reviewer has never had a product, the explanation of what's good and bad about it will be limited. If a review sounds more like a product manual than a real-life experience, it probably is.

7 Use of language

Some dishonest companies will provide templates for their "reviewers" to make it easier for quick copying and pasting. If you see the same or similar words and phrases in different reviews, be suspicious. Reviews with words like "best thing ever" and "worst thing ever" without any explanation are likely to be created from a template.

8 When haters start to love

A common form of fake review is for the reviewer to insist that they hated a product but were given one as a gift and they suddenly discovered it's the best thing since sliced bread. Also look for a lot of question marks and exclamation points. "Why didn't I buy this sooner??? I love it!!!!!!"

9 All or nothing

Fake reviews tend to be either one star or five stars. Make sure you check reviews at two, three, and four stars, too – real reviews tend to be more moderate.

B | GROUP WORK | THINK CRITICALLY | Why do you think people write fake reviews? Which tips from the article have you used or might you try in the future to identify fake reviews? Can you think of more tips for identifying them?

INSIDER ENGLISH

Say *the best* or *greatest thing since sliced bread* to describe extremely useful and important things.

2 WRITING

A **Read part of an essay. What's the author's position? What research and example are given?**

Are product reviews useful or not?

Although many people don't trust product reviews, **I strongly believe that** they are useful. You can't trust advertisements to … However, you can trust honest reviewers to … It's very easy to read reviews before you buy to help you …

Reviews are valuable because they give you a genuine picture of … **Research shows that** 84 percent of people trust online reviewers as much as they trust their friends. This is because … **One time I** wanted to a buy a toaster, so I read several reviews on the product. I found out … This was helpful because … Mistakes can be avoided if you read reviews first.

While it's true that many reviews aren't authentic, it's easy to figure out whether they're fake or not. You can … You can also … Reviews must not be ignored because … If you read a large number of reviews for a product, it helps you … The benefits are more numerous than the problems.

In conclusion, **I feel that** reviews help us make better decisions. They give us a true idea … Many are … , and it's not difficult to … Read reviews to avoid bad purchases.

B **USE PERSUASIVE LANGUAGE** **Read about how to write a persuasive essay. Add the bold expressions in the essay in exercise 2A to the examples of persuasive language below. Then, in pairs, think of ideas to complete the essay.**

In a persuasive essay, your aim is to convince your reader to agree with your view. It usually has three or four paragraphs:

Introduction: State your position on the topic.

Body (one or two paragraphs): Support your position with facts and examples. You can also state the opposite position and say why it is not true.

Conclusion: Restate your position and main points. Give a strong concluding statement to make your reader agree with you.

Useful persuasive language:

Give your opinion: I firmly believe that … , _____ … , _____ …

Give facts: According to … , _____ …

Give personal examples: When I used/tried … , _____ …

Give the opposite position: Although some will say that … , _____ … , _____ …

C **PLAN** **You're going to write a persuasive essay. Work with a partner. Choose one of the options below, and discuss your ideas. Then plan the structure of your essay: What opening sentence are you going to use? What information are you going to include in each of the paragraphs listed in exercise 2B?**

> Are   product reviews / restaurant reviews / movie reviews / app reviews / hotel reviews   useful or not?

D **Write your persuasive essay. Make sure you use some persuasive language.**

E **PAIR WORK** **Exchange essays with another partner. Do you agree with the writer's position?**

TIME TO SPEAK
Does it really work?

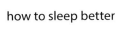

how to cure a cough

how to sleep better

how to keep mosquitos away

how to remove coffee stains

how to fix a wet phone

A **PREPARE** With a partner, look at things people searched for on the internet. Discuss examples of tips the searches might find. Talk about any you have tried and say how effective they were.

how to cure a cough	how to sleep better
how to keep mosquitos away	how to cool soda quickly
how to remove coffee stains	how to get in shape in a month
how to fix a wet phone	

FIND IT

B **RESEARCH** With your partner, think of a few other tips you have heard of or tried. You can choose two or three topics from the ideas in part A or use your phone to check for ideas online. The tips can be effective or ineffective.

C **DISCUSS** In groups, share your topics and tips. The others guess which ones are effective. If you have tried any of the tips, at the end of the discussion, say how effective they were. The group chooses two of the most interesting tips: an effective one and an ineffective one.

D **PRESENT** In your groups from part C, present your two tips to the class without mentioning the problems they solve. The class guesses what the problems are. Then each group reveals the answers.

E **DECIDE** As a class, discuss whether the tips you heard are effective or not and say whether you've tried any.

To check your progress, go to page 156.

USEFUL PHRASES

PREPARE	**DISCUSS**	**PRESENT**
I've tried that before and …	… , believe it or not.	According to … ,
… seems like a great tip.	I find that hard to believe.	The best way to … is …
… can't be true.	It's partly true.	In order to …
That just doesn't sound right.	Maybe there's some truth in it.	It turns out, if you …
	Tell me another one!	

UNIT OBJECTIVES
- talk about talent
- discuss how to make life better
- describe your ambitions
- write a review of a performance
- give a presentation about yourself

GOT WHAT IT TAKES?

12

START SPEAKING

A   What can you see in the picture? Why do you think the person chose to learn this skill?

B   What skills or characteristics do you think a person needs to have to be good at the activity in the picture?

C   In your opinion, what does it take to be highly successful – whatever you choose to do in life? For ideas, watch Wendy's video.

EXPERT SPEAKER

Are any of Wendy's ideas similar to yours?

1 LANGUAGE IN CONTEXT

A **PAIR WORK** Look at the picture. How long do you think it took the person to learn to do this? Talk about an activity you know about that takes a lot of practice to do well.

B Read the social media posts. What is the 10,000-hour rule? What talents and skills are mentioned?

••• ‹ ›

Comments 🔘 Profile 🔄 Sign Out

Victor Gomez
I just read about the 10,000-hour rule: You have to practice something for 10,000 hours to become truly good at it. It made me wonder if anyone is really born **gifted** or if ability just comes from being **determined** and working really hard. Thoughts? 👍 💬

Rhonda Peters
Jimi Hendrix was one of the greatest guitarists in history, but he never took guitar lessons. So, if he wasn't a **trained** musician, then you figure he was just exceptionally **talented**. But it's not necessarily true that his natural **musical** ability was the only factor. When he got his first guitar at age 15, he practiced for hours and hours every day. So he didn't play especially well at first. It takes practice to become a **skilled** musician, no matter what natural talent you may have. 👍 💬

Kyle Manson
I'm studying engineering, and some of my classes are technically advanced, but I pick up the ideas fairly easily. Others are having real difficulty, even though I'm no smarter than they are and they work as hard as I do. Design classes are where I struggle. I'm reasonably **imaginative**, but I'm definitely a **technical**, **analytical** person, not **artistic** at all. I can make a diagram of a complicated structure like a bridge without much effort, but drawing never came particularly easily to me. So we're studying the same things, but we're each better in different classes. The only **logical** explanation is natural ability. That's my (analytical) conclusion! 👍 💬

C Read again. How do Rhonda and Kyle feel about practice versus being born with talent?

2 VOCABULARY: Skill and performance

FIND IT

A 🔊 **2.45** Look at the adjectives in the box used to describe talents and skills. Which of them are used in the posts in exercise 1B? Count the syllables in the words and guess where the main stress is. Discuss their meanings. Use a dictionary or your phone to help you. Then listen and check your work.

analytical	artistic	athletic	competent	determined	gifted	imaginative
intellectual	logical	musical	skilled	talented	technical	trained

B ➤ Now go to page 152. Do the vocabulary exercises for 12.1.

C **PAIR WORK** **THINK CRITICALLY** Do you think very successful people are born gifted, or is their talent due to practice? For ideas, watch Wendy's video.

EXPERT SPEAKER

Do you think Wendy is right? Can you think of other examples?

3 GRAMMAR: Adverbs with adjectives and adverbs

A **Read the sentences in the grammar box. Answer the questions.**

> ### Adverbs with adjectives and adverbs
>
> You have to practice something for 10,000 hours to become **truly good** at it.
> But it's not **necessarily true**.
> So he didn't play **especially well** at first.
> Drawing never came **particularly easily** to me.

1 What part of speech can you use with an adjective or an adverb to provide more detail about it? _____

2 Is it placed before or after the adjective or adverb it modifies? _____

B ▶ **Now go to page 139. Look at the grammar chart and do the grammar exercise for 12.1.**

C **Write something about yourself that is true for each topic below. Use adverbs with adjectives or adverbs. Then work with a partner. Guess what your partner's sentence might be. Then compare your answers.**

1 Cooking: _____   **4** Money: _____

2 Technology: _____   **5** Decision-making: _____

3 Fixing things: _____   _____

4 SPEAKING

A GROUP WORK **Think about your experiences in these areas and discuss the questions. Did you ever (a) find it especially easy to become good at something because of natural talent, (b) find it particularly difficult or impossible to accomplish something even with practice, or (c) become good at something through practice even though it was difficult at first?**

art (painting, drawing, photography, etc.)   athletic activities (soccer, yoga, running, etc.)
education (math, language learning, computers, etc.)   performance (singing, playing an instrument, dancing, etc.)

> I think I'm **exceptionally skilled** with technology. For example, **technical** issues with my computer are easy for me to understand and fix. But I've never been **artistically gifted**. I took an art class, but I couldn't even do a simple drawing of a bowl of fruit.

1 LANGUAGE IN CONTEXT

A 🔊 **2.46** Imagine you have to give a short talk on how to make the world a better place. What would you talk about? Then read and listen to Pietro giving a talk at a conference. Circle the best title for his talk.

a Big Ideas for a Better World

b A Better World for Everyone

c Think of Others before Yourself

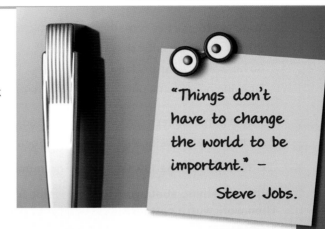

"Things don't have to change the world to be important." – Steve Jobs.

🔊 **2.46 Audio script**

Hello! Wow, thank you for that warm welcome. It really makes me smile! I actually smile a lot these days, but that wasn't always the case. In fact, meeting me used to **be a real downer**. I know this because a good friend told me so. She said seeing me would instantly **ruin her day** because I was always complaining about something. She told me that my negative attitude **was getting her down**. Well, that was a shock, but it **did me good** because it showed me that I needed to change.

I started doing small, simple things to **raise my spirits**. Listening to a great piece of music while getting dressed. Having a cup of coffee and a cookie in the afternoon, just because. Changing my desktop wallpaper to a beautiful work of art. Sticking an inspirational quote or a great piece of advice on the fridge so it was the first thing I saw every morning.

Then I used the same idea – small, simple things – to help **brighten up** other people's lives. Just simple acts of kindness, like cooking a meal for my mom, driving my elderly neighbor to her friend's place, or offering a few words of encouragement to my younger brother for something he was doing. A little bit of kindness can really **make someone's day** and **leave a lasting impression on** them and on you.

So here's my big idea for how to change the world – think small. By all of us doing small things, we all collectively make the world a better place.

B 🔊 **2.46** Read and listen again. How does Pietro suggest making (a) yourself happy and (b) others happy? In your opinion, what's Pietro's best idea? Why?

2 VOCABULARY: Describing emotional impact

FIND IT

A 🔊 **2.47** PAIR WORK Look at the expressions in the box. Which describe a positive impact, a negative impact, or both? Use a dictionary or your phone to help you. Then listen and check your work.

be a (real) downer	brighten up sth	capture sb's imagination
do sb good	get sb down	leave a lasting impression on sb
make sb's day	put sb's mind at rest	raise sb's spirits
ruin sb's day	stress sb out	take sb's mind off sth

B ▶ Now go to page 152. Do the vocabulary exercises for 12.2.

C PAIR WORK THINK CRITICALLY Talk about examples of people's behavior that affect you negatively and positively.

3 GRAMMAR: Making non-count nouns countable

A **Read the sentences in the grammar box. Circle the correct options to complete the rules.**

> ### Making non-count nouns countable
>
> Listen to **a** great **piece of music** while getting dressed.
>
> Have **a cup of coffee** and **a cookie** in the afternoon.
>
> Change my desktop wallpaper to **a** beautiful **work of art**.
>
> Stick an inspirational quote or **a** great **piece of advice** on the fridge.
>
> **A little bit of kindness** can really make someone's day.

1 You can make non-count nouns countable by using expressions that describe specific **qualities or characteristics /
quantities or amounts**.

2 **Sometimes you can / You can never** use the same noun (e.g., piece) with different categories of things.

B ▶ **Now go to page 140. Look at the grammar chart and do the grammar exercise for 12.2.**

C **Complete the sentences with your own ideas. Check
your accuracy. Then compare ideas with a partner.
Are they similar?**

1 One of my favorite pieces of _____ is
_____ .

2 I think _____ is a really nice
act of _____ .

3 I once got a very useful piece of _____ from a
friend. It was: _____ .

4 I'd really like to get a bunch of _____ together for a game of _____ .

5 I never have enough articles of _____ ! I need some more _____ .

6 I sometimes go out for _____ to brighten up my day.

> ✓ **ACCURACY** CHECK
>
> **When making non-count nouns countable,
> be sure the subject and verb agree.**
>
> *All of the ~~piece~~ of advice he gave were useful.* ✗
> *All of the pieces of advice he gave were useful.* ✓

4 SPEAKING

A **PAIR WORK** **THINK CRITICALLY** **Think of more small things you can do to make the world a better place for
yourself and others. Explain why they're good ideas. Make a list.**

> Well, one way to **make someone's day** is to give them a gift for no reason.
> Maybe **a box of** Turkish **delight** or some flowers.

> Nice one! And if someone's stressed, you could suggest a day trip
> together to **take their mind off things** – or maybe **a game of** soccer.

B **GROUP WORK** **Share your ideas and reasons with another pair. Then choose the two best ideas that the other
pair suggested.**

Turkish delight

12.3   MAYBE ONE DAY ...

1 LISTENING

A **PAIR WORK**   Daniel is interviewing to get into a theater program in college. What do you think the interviewer asks him about?

B 🔊 **2.48** Listen to the interview. What does the interviewer ask about? Were your guesses in exercise 1A correct?

C 🔊 **2.48**   **LISTEN FOR CONTRASTING IDEAS**   Listen again and match Daniel's optimistic ideas with his cautious ones.

1 My dream scenario is to play leading roles. ____

2 There's no guarantee I'll end up in Hollywood. ____

3 I may not succeed in playing any type of character. ____

4 It may not be easy to learn new things. ____

a But there's no harm in trying.

b But I realize things might not go as planned.

c But I'm determined to be open-minded and try everything.

d But I'm confident that I'll have some level of success.

D **PAIR WORK**   **THINK CRITICALLY**   How realistic do you think Daniel's ambitions are? What do you think of his attitude during the interview? Does he have the right attitude to be an actor? Explain.

2 PRONUNCIATION: Listening for sounds that change

A 🔊 **2.49** Listen to how the /d/ sound changes in connected speech.

Well, my dream scenario would be to play leading roles in movies. (/d/ → /b/)

Listen to examples of how other sounds change:

I think she had the best part in the film. (/t/ → /p/)

There were only seven people in the theater. (/n/ → /m/)

I met one guy who had been in Hollywood. (/n/ → /ŋ/)   (/d/ → /b/)

B 🔊 **2.50** Work in pairs. Mark the possible sound changes at the end of words. Listen and check.

1 I love that part where the son meets his real father.

2 They arrived before everyone came.

3 The movie had bad reviews on most websites.

4 It was an action movie set in Greece.

C Circle the correct options to complete the sentence.

In connected speech, words that *start / end* in /t/, /d/, and /n/ can change before words *starting / ending* in /p/, /b/, /m/, /k/, and /g/.

3 SPEAKING SKILLS

A 🔊 **2.48** Complete the expressions from the interview in exercise 1B on page 122 with the words in the box. Then decide which ones are used to (a) describe ambitions, (b) express optimism, or (c) express caution. Write *a*, *b*, or *c* next to each one. Will any of the sounds change in these expressions in connected speech? If so, which ones? Listen again to check.

certain	confident	determined	guarantee	harm	planned	reason	scenario	ultimate

Describe ambitions; express optimism and caution

1 My dream _____ would be to …
2 I realize things might not go as _____ .
3 There's no _____ (that) …
4 I'm _____ (that) …
5 My _____ goal is to …

6 There's no _____ in trying.
7 I can't say for _____ (that) …
8 I'm _____ to …
9 I see no _____ why I can't …

B **PAIR WORK** Choose one of the situations below and interview your partner about their ambitions. Use expressions from exercise 3A and your own ideas. Then choose a different situation and change roles.

attending a music school	attending law school	being on a reality TV show
getting an internship at a museum	working as an English teacher	volunteering at a hospital

4 PRONUNCIATION: Using syllable stress in words

A 🔊 **2.51** Listen to which syllable is stressed (a stressed syllable is said more loudly, longer, and at a higher pitch).

ul̲timate   guaran̲tee   scena̲rio

B 🔊 **2.52** Which syllable is stressed in these words? Complete the chart. Listen, check, and repeat the words.

character	difficulties	encouragement	impression	interviewer	particular
performance	photograph	photography	positively	successful	technical

⬤ • • **com̲petent**	• ⬤ • **deter̲mined**	⬤ • • • **sa̲tisfying**	• ⬤ • • **excep̲tional**

C 🔊 **2.53** Complete the conversation with the word that matches the stress pattern. Listen and check your work. Practice the conversation with a partner.

I think Maria is such a ⬤ • • *hard-working / positive* person. She's • ⬤ • • *amazingly / wonderfully* talented.

Max is quite • ⬤ • *creative / competent*, too. He did this ⬤ • • • *incredible / complicated* work so well.

5 SPEAKING

A **PAIR WORK** Think of one or two of your ambitions – educational, personal, or professional. Then ask each other what you need to do to achieve the ambitions and how difficult it will be. Explain, expressing optimistic and cautious opinions.

> I'm **determined to** become an architect. My **ultimate goal is to** improve my city. I'll need a lot of training, but I'm **confident** I can manage it.

12.4 SUCCESS BEHIND THE SCENES

1 READING

A **Who helps make a concert successful in addition to the musicians? Read the article. What were Kevin's job responsibilities? What does he think was difficult about the job?**

BACKSTAGE PASS

I loved life on the road when I was a guitar tech. Over the years, I traveled with many different bands – some small acts and some big stars. My job included unloading the equipment, setting it up on stage, tuning guitars, and making sure everything worked – pretty much getting things ready so the musicians could perform without problems in front of a bunch of excited fans.

When I was about eight years old, I saw the Rolling Stones perform on TV. I noticed that someone handed Keith Richards a guitar between songs, and I thought I'd like to do that one day. It left a lasting impression on me, but I didn't really think about the job again until I was 25. That's when a friend asked me to travel with his band as a guitar tech. I already knew a lot about music and guitars, but on the job, I really became technically skilled over time. People hired me by word of mouth, mostly musicians from headlining acts that we were touring with. I quickly had several jobs on my résumé – but it's really more of a see-and-be-seen business. You look at the people around you and see what jobs might be coming up. And you do your job exceptionally well every day – others see you work, know your skill set, and often ask you to work for them on future shows.

I enjoyed the pressure of live performances, but life on the road wasn't always easy. You take the good with the bad. Sometimes I slept in vans and sometimes on tour buses. When I stayed in hotels, they weren't necessarily nice, but with some of the more-famous musicians, we were in beautiful hotels, like the time I stayed on the Champs-Élysées in Paris. I worked in several different cities around the world, and dealing with the unknown often made the job especially challenging. A lot of times I was working outside, and it could be very hot, really cold, or even raining. I also dealt with things like getting big trucks down tiny streets and getting huge equipment up narrow stairs or in small elevators. One time, in Malaga, Spain, the power went out in the entire city, and it messed up our schedule and computers, but the show went ahead as planned.

Any type of work in the music business is difficult. I've seen musicians on the way up, and I've seen them on the way down. It's tough to get to the top in my line of work, too, but the work is steadier once you're successful. And how do you stay at the top? Start with being on time. Then stay focused, and always remember you're not in the band. You're there to do a job – not to hang out with rock stars. I've seen a lot of techs make that mistake.

My last words of advice? I think there are three kinds of people in this world: (1) the kind that make things happen, (2) the kind that watch things happen, and (3) the kind that wonder what just happened. Be the kind of person that makes things happen. And remember, no matter what happens – the show must go on!

 by Kevin Hurdman

GLOSSARY

unload (*v*) remove something from a vehicle
headlining act (*n*) the main performer or performers at an entertainment event
steadier (*adj*) happening in a more regular way than something else

B **UNDERSTAND CAUSE AND EFFECT** **Read the article again. What is/was the result of these events?**

1 Kevin got everything ready for the performance.
2 Kevin saw someone give Keith Richards a guitar on TV.
3 The power went out in Malaga before a concert.
4 You do your job exceptionally well.

C **PAIR WORK** **THINK CRITICALLY** **In what other types of jobs is it helpful to "see and be seen"? What other advice does Kevin give that can be applied to different jobs?**

A   Read the concert review from an online music magazine. What did the reviewer like? Did anything go wrong?

CONCERT REVIEW | ALEJANDRO SANZ

The Alejandro Sanz concert on Friday night was amazing. He's from Spain and tours all over the world. I was fortunate to see him in New York City at a sold-out show. He was the headlining act and sang exceptionally well. The band members were from Puerto Rico, the Dominican Republic, and the United States. The drummer was particularly good. They played mostly songs from his newest albums, but they also played some old favorites.

The show was a huge success due to the talented musicians, but it wasn't only their work that made it so special. The lighting and special effects were terrific, so the behind-the-scenes crew clearly did a great job, making sure everything ran smoothly and that there were no technical problems. And I loved the video clips on the giant screen at the back of the stage. It all helped to make the concert feel spectacular.

But the best part was when Sanz sang "Corazón Partío" and had the audience sing along. Everyone was disappointed when the show was over, and they shouted for more. As a result, Sanz performed an encore, which really made our day.

GLOSSARY

encore (*n*) an extra song or piece of music played at the end of a show because the audience shouts for it

B   **SHOW REASON AND RESULT** Look at the sentences with words that show reasons and results. Find one more expression for each sentence from the review in exercise 2A.

The show was a huge success **because of /** [1] _____ the talented musicians.

They shouted for more. **Consequently / Therefore /** [2] _____ , Sanz performed an encore, which really made our day.

WRITE IT

C   **PLAN** You are going to write a review of a performance. With a partner, talk about a concert, play, or other performance you have seen. Discuss facts about the events and information about your experience: where and when it was; what you liked and didn't like about the performers, lighting, sound, and special effects. Then look at the concert review in exercise 2A. How will you organize the information you discussed?

D   Write your performance review. Remember to use expressions for showing reason and result.

E   **PAIR WORK** Read your partner's review. Would you have liked the event? Why or why not?

REGISTER CHECK

In conversation, *so* is often used instead of more formal expressions like *as a result*, *consequently*, and *therefore*. It's used to join two sentences.

Formal writing

*They shouted for more. **As a result**, Sanz performed an encore.*

Conversation

*We shouted for more, **so** Sanz performed an encore.*

TIME TO SPEAK
Me, in two minutes

A Choose three items that you always carry in your purse or bag. You can think about the apps on your phone that you never do without, if you like. Show them to your partner or group, or describe them. What do they show about you? (For example, your personality, hobbies or interests, or what you focus on each day.) Who has the most unusual items? Whose are the most revealing?

B Look at the mood board above. What objects and text can you identify? What does it tell you about the person who created the mood board? How does the person see themselves? What are their aspirations and dreams?

C **PREPARE** Now you're going to expand on how you described yourself in exercise A. Work with your partner to design a mood board for each of you. What objects and texts are on your boards? Why? To help you, look at the list of categories below and choose the ones that are relevant to you or use your own ideas.

current/past jobs	future plans/ambitions	childhood	family	friends
interests	personal ambitions	personality	challenges	skills

D Describe your mood board. What can your partner tell about you from the items you've chosen to include?

E Imagine you're going to talk about yourself for two minutes. Using your mood board, work alone to plan what you're going to say about yourself. Choose the best order to present your topics or areas of interest, and use examples to illustrate each topic.

F **DISCUSS** In groups, take turns talking about yourselves. Then say what aspects of each person's talk you liked (e.g., examples, topics, timing, body language / gestures, tone of voice). What lessons did you learn on how to talk about yourself in an interesting way?

G **AGREE** Share your ideas from part D with the class. Agree on a short list of tips on the most interesting way to talk about yourself (topics, sequence, etc.).

To check your progress, go to page 156.

USEFUL PHRASES

PREPARE

I'm determined to …

I'm fairly talented at …

I'm more analytical/artistic/…

My ultimate goal is to …

AGREE

You could try …

It might work well if you …

… could be very effective.

I've always had luck with …

REVIEW 4 (UNITS 10–12)

1 VOCABULARY

A   Complete the questions with the correct forms of the words in parentheses ( ). Sometimes, you do not need to change the word.

1   These days, do children really need to learn to do _____ (calculate) without a calculator?

2   If you think an email is suspicious, how can you check that it's _____ (authentic)?

3   Are there many _____ (similar) between your native language and English?

4   Is there a _____ (like) between you and anyone famous?

5   Is asking people to fill out forms a good way to _____ (survey) customers?

6   In your country, are there any snakes or insects whose bites are _____ (dead)?

7   To be an _____ (art) person, do you need to be born with a natural talent?

8   Is it true that most jobs require people to be _____ (imagine) in some way?

9   If you do something that you didn't know was _____ (legal), should you be punished?

10   Is it good to change your _____ (look) completely sometimes?

B   PAIR WORK   Discuss the questions in exercise 1A.

2 GRAMMAR

A   Circle the correct option.

1   Carrying your phone in your back pocket increases the risk *to break* / *of breaking* it.

2   When you apologize *to arrive* / *for arriving* late, you should always explain why you're late.

3   If I drink coffee in the evening, it prevents me *to sleep* / *from sleeping*.

4   People in my country learn English particularly *easy* / *easily* because it's similar to our language.

5   They should allow people *take* / *to take* phones into exams as long as they are put away.

6   Companies should let their employees *wear* / *to wear* what they want at work.

7   I've listened to my favorite piece *from* / *of* music at least 100 times.

8   Most *exceptional* / *exceptionally* gifted people discover their talent before they're 18.

9   It's always easy to find stuff online to help you *understand* / *understanding* difficult subjects.

10   I sometimes dream *to become* / *of becoming* famous.

11   I have one article *of* / *in* clothing that I wear much more often than any other.

12   Traffic jams cause me *arrive* / *to arrive* late more than any other problem.

B   PAIR WORK   Do you agree or disagree with the sentences in exercise 2A? Discuss your views.

3 VOCABULARY

A (Circle) the correct options.

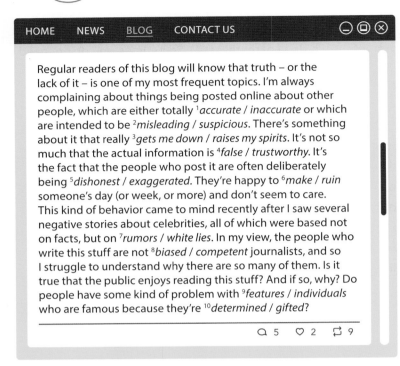

| HOME | NEWS | BLOG | CONTACT US |

Regular readers of this blog will know that truth – or the lack of it – is one of my most frequent topics. I'm always complaining about things being posted online about other people, which are either totally ¹*accurate / inaccurate* or which are intended to be ²*misleading / suspicious*. There's something about it that really ³*gets me down / raises my spirits*. It's not so much that the actual information is ⁴*false / trustworthy*. It's the fact that the people who post it are often deliberately being ⁵*dishonest / exaggerated*. They're happy to ⁶*make / ruin* someone's day (or week, or more) and don't seem to care. This kind of behavior came to mind recently after I saw several negative stories about celebrities, all of which were based not on facts, but on ⁷*rumors / white lies*. In my view, the people who write this stuff are not ⁸*biased / competent* journalists, and so I struggle to understand why there are so many of them. Is it true that the public enjoys reading this stuff? And if so, why? Do people have some kind of problem with ⁹*features / individuals* who are famous because they're ¹⁰*determined / gifted*?

💬 5 ♡ 2 ↻ 9

B **PAIR WORK** **Say whether or not you agree with the views in the blog in exercise 3A. Discuss the questions at the end.**

4 GRAMMAR

A **Complete the sentences with the correct form of *be*.**

1 All my work will _____ finished by the end of this week.

2 All my photos _____ stored on my phone.

3 I have some old stuff that needs _____ thrown out.

4 Most of the English words I know _____ learned in the classroom.

5 I always feel nervous when I'm _____ interviewed.

6 A lot of the things I say shouldn't _____ taken seriously.

7 I ordered something online, and it hasn't _____ delivered yet.

8 When I _____ delayed by traffic, I never get stressed about it.

9 Once, one of my online accounts _____ hacked.

10 Next weekend, all my time is going _____ spent relaxing.

11 I once saw a car that was _____ chased by the police.

12 I expect _____ invited to a party fairly soon.

B **PAIR WORK** **Say which sentences from exercise 4A are true for you. For ones that are not, say a similar sentence that is true.**

GRAMMAR REFERENCE AND PRACTICE

7.1 GERUNDS AND INFINITIVES AFTER ADJECTIVES, NOUNS, AND PRONOUNS (PAGE 67)

Gerunds and infinitives after adjectives, nouns, and pronouns

Infinitives (*to* + verb)	**Gerunds** (verb + *-ing*)
1 Adjective + infinitive ***It's boring and difficult to work*** *at night.*	**1** Adjective + gerund *It was **boring waiting** in line for the roller coaster. But it was **cool riding** on it.*
2 Noun + infinitive – to show purpose *It was an interesting **place to visit**.*	**2** Fixed expression + gerund e.g.: *be worth, have fun, spend/waste time*
3 Pronoun + infinitive – to show purpose *I need **something to eat**.*	*I **spend a lot of time traveling*** *for my job.*

A **Circle the correct options. More than one answer may be possible.**

I start work at 6:00 a.m. It's hard ¹*to get / getting* up so early, and I usually don't want to spend time ²*to make / making* breakfast, but I try to have something simple ³*to eat / eating*. At least I have no trouble ⁴*to get / getting* to work, as I don't waste time ⁵*to sit / sitting* in traffic jams. I think that's a big advantage ⁶*to have / having*.

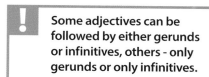

! Some adjectives can be followed by either gerunds or infinitives, others - only gerunds or only infinitives.

7.2 INFINITIVES AFTER VERBS WITH AND WITHOUT OBJECTS (PAGE 69)

Infinitives after verbs with and without objects

1 Verb + infinitive Common verbs: *agree, decide, hope, manage, plan, seem, tend*
*They **agreed not to climb** the mountain without an instructor.*

2 Verb + object + infinitive Common verbs: *allow, convince, encourage, teach, tell, urge, warn*
*He **did not convince us to hire** him.* (The object performs the action of the infinitive.)

3 Verb + (object) + infinitive Common verbs: *ask, expect, need, promise, want, would like*
- No object – subject performs the action of the infinitive
- With object – object performs the action of the infinitive

*I'd **like to buy** the lamp. (I'm buying it.)* *I'd **like you to buy** that lamp. (You're buying it.)*

! Use *not* before the infinitive to show the infinitive is negative. Use *not* before the main verb to show it is negative.

A **Which of these sentences are correct without an object? Add the object in parentheses ( ) where possible.**

1 I like to shop online. (you)
2 I'd like to move closer to my dad. (my sister)
3 Jack tends to forget his friends' birthdays. (them)
4 My parents advised to save money. (me)
5 You convinced to buy a new computer. (them)
6 They expect to get good grades. (her)

8.1 MODAL-LIKE EXPRESSIONS WITH *BE* (PAGE 77)

Modal-like expressions with *be*

1   *Be bound to / Be certain to / Be sure to* for things that are definitely going to happen
    *If you drop that glass, it's **bound to** / **certain to** / **sure to** break.*

2   *Be likely/unlikely to* for things that are probably (not) going to happen
    *There's a lot of traffic, so we're **likely to** be late.*

3   *Be supposed to* for things expected to happen (because they were arranged or sb is responsible for them)
    *My mom **was supposed to** pick me up at 3:30, but she didn't arrive until 4:00.*

4   *Be about to* for things that you're going to do soon or are going to happen soon
    *Quick, turn on the TV. The game **is about to** start.*

5   *Be required to* for things that we are made to do (e.g., because of rules)
    *Everyone who travels by plane **is required to** have a passport or some kind of photo ID.*

6   *Be forced to* for things that we are made to do, but don't want to
    *I missed the last bus, so I **was forced to** walk home.*

7   *Be allowed to / Be permitted to* for things that we have permission to do
    *They're **allowed to** / **permitted to** use their phones in school, but not in class.*

A   **Circle the correct option.**

1   The president just came into the room, so I think she's *about to / unlikely to* start her speech.
2   He hardly went to any classes, so he was *bound to / about to* do badly on the exam.
3   My coworker was off from work all week, so I was *sure to / forced to* do two jobs – mine and his.
4   We were *allowed to / required to* give our passport numbers when we checked into the hotel.
5   Only people who bought tickets online were *forced to / permitted to* go into the theater.
6   They're *about to / supposed to* announce the exam results in six weeks.

8.2 FUTURE FORMS (PAGE 79)

Future forms

1   Present continuous: for general future intentions and definite plans or
    arrangements *I'm **making** a film about college life.*
    *I'm **meeting** my friends tomorrow at 6:00 p.m.*

2   *Be going to*: for general future plans and intention and predictions about the
    future *I'm **going to make** a film about college life.*
    *It's **going to be** a big surprise for them.*

3   *Might, may,* or *could*: when you're not sure about the future
    *I **might start** my own business one day.*

4   *Will*: for predictions about the future and decisions made at the moment of speaking
    *It **will be** a big surprise for them.*
    *That looks difficult. I'**ll help** you with it.*

5   *Will + be* + verb + *-ing* (the future continuous): for an action in progress at a future time and for plans
    and intentions
    *In a few years, I'**ll be looking** for a job.*
    ***Will** you **be coming** to the meeting on Thursday?*

! The future continuous and *be going to* can both express future plans and intentions. The future continuous is more formal.

A **Complete the conversation with the verbs in parentheses ( ) in appropriate future forms.**

A I'm not sure yet, but I ¹_____ (ask) Juan for help. Do you know if he ²_____ (come) out with us tonight?

B No. He ³_____ (not, leave) the office yet. He's so busy these days! He ⁴_____ (get) sick unless he takes it easy.

A No. I think he ⁵_____ (be) fine. His vacation starts next month, so soon he ⁶_____ (relax) on a beach somewhere.

9.1 UNREAL CONDITIONALS (PAGE 87)

> **Unreal conditionals**
>
> **Present and future**
>
> *if* clause: *could*, simple past, or past continuous (imagined situation)
> result clause: *would/could/might* + base form of a verb (predicted or possible result)
> **If** Josh **was/were studying** at the library, I **could help** him with his homework.
> **If** we **got / could get** tickets to the concert, we **wouldn't watch** it on TV.
>
> **Past**
>
> *if* clause: past perfect (something possible that did not happen)
> result clause: *would/could/may/might have* + past participle (imaginary past result that didn't happen)
> I **could have been** an X-ray technician **if** I **had studied** medicine.
> Or *would* + base form of a verb (imaginary present result)
> I **would have** a nicer apartment **if** I **hadn't bought** a new car.

A **Complete the sentences with the correct form of the words in parentheses.**

1 If Brenda was trying out for that play, she _____ (get) a good part.

2 I would take a dance class if I _____ (not hurt) my ankle.

3 I _____ (change) jobs if I could, but I can't right now.

4 If I had gotten to the restaurant later, I _____ (not see) my cousin.

5 If I had heard the news, I _____ (be) at your house right now.

6 If they _____ (work) fewer hours, they wouldn't be so tired.

9.2 WISHES AND REGRETS (PAGE 89)

> **Wishes and regrets**
>
> *I wish (that) / If only* express a wish for something to be different or feelings of regret.
>
> 1 For wishes about general situations in the present: *I wish / If only* + simple past
> *I wish / If only I knew* the answer to this question.
>
> 2 For wishes about continuous situations in the present: *I wish / If only* + past continuous
> *I wish / If only I was/were sitting* at home and not in this traffic jam.
>
> 3 For wishes about ability or possibility in the present: *I wish / If only* + could/couldn't
> *I wish / If only I could* find that book.
>
> 4 For wishes about situations in the past: *I wish / If only* + past perfect
> *I wish / If only I had bought* tickets in advance.
>
> **!** After *I wish / If only*, you can use *was* (informal) or *were* (more formal) with *I, he, she,* and *it.*

A **Complete the conversation.**

Jose Wow, it's hot on this bus! I wish it ¹_____ ten degrees cooler.

Ed If only we ²_____ buy some cold sodas.

Jose Yeah, this water's warm. I wish I ³_____ the bottle in the refrigerator last night.

Ed Right now, I wish I ⁴_____ in a refrigerator! If only the air conditioning ⁵_____ broken!

137

10.1 GERUNDS AFTER PREPOSITIONS (PAGE 99)

Gerunds after prepositions

1 Verb + preposition + gerund (e.g., *boast about, care about, insist on, plan on, result in, think of, worry about*)
   Josh **boasted about buying** a new car.

2 *be* + adjective + preposition + gerund (e.g., *be afraid of, be excited about, be guilty of, be interested in*)
   We **are guilty of spending** too much time on social media.

3 Noun + *of* + gerund (e.g., *benefits, cost, danger, fear, idea, importance, possibility, process, risk, way*)
   My **fear of flying** has stopped me from visiting you.

A **Complete the sentences with the gerund form of the correct words.**

develop	do	recycle	try	win	work

1 Mia often complains about _____ on the weekends.
2 What are the benefits of _____ plastic?
3 Larry isn't afraid of _____ unusual foods.
4 The soccer team succeeded in _____ every game this season.
5 I'm guilty of _____ the same thing instead of trying new things.
6 You need to concentrate on _____ your plan before you can start a business.

10.2 CAUSATIVE VERBS (PAGE 101)

Causative verbs

1 *Help/let/make/have* + object + base form of the verb   *My parents **make me save** money for my future.*
2 *Allow/cause/enable* + object + infinitive   *Surveys **enable stores to estimate** sales.*
3 *Keep/prevent/protect/stop* + object + *from* + gerund   *Her advice **kept me from losing** my job.*

A **Complete the sentences with the words in parentheses ( ) in the correct form. Add *from* when necessary.**

1 Customer feedback frequently _____ our products. (make, we, improve)
2 We tried to _____ too much money, but we failed. (prevent, he, spend)
3 Having my own home has _____ independent. (enable, I, be)
4 After a business trip, I usually _____ an extra day off. (let, my team, take)
5 My computer is broken, which has _____ any work done. (keep, I, get)
6 Worrying about his business _____ a lot of weight last year. (cause, he, lose)

11.1 PASSIVE FORMS (PAGE 109)

Passive forms

Passive and active sentences have similar meanings. But in the passive, the receiver of the action is more important than the doer and becomes the subject of the sentence. Add *by* + the agent if necessary.

1 Simple present passive: *am/is/are* + past participle   *These products **are** usually **imported**.*
2 Simple past passive: *was/were* + past participle   ***Were** you **given** a refund?*
3 Present perfect passive: *has/have been* + past participle   *The order **has been canceled**.*
4 Future passive: *am/is/are going to/will* + *be* + past participle   *The goods **will be checked** before they're shipped.*
5 Present continuous passive: *am/is/are* + *being* + past participle   *Many goods **are being imported**.*
6 Past continuous passive: *was/were* + *being* + past participle   *The store **wasn't being used** until now.*

Rewrite the sentences in the passive form. Add *by* + the agent if it's important.

1 We won't solve the problem of counterfeit goods easily . _____
2 A man found illegal copies of movies and games in a garage. _____
3 They're going to debate the issue of fake goods on TV. _____
4 For a long time, people were selling fake goods openly in markets. _____
5 Recently, they've changed the laws on counterfeit goods. _____
6 The government is now watching traders more carefully. _____

11.2 PASSIVES WITH MODALS AND MODAL-LIKE EXPRESSIONS; PASSIVE INFINITIVES (PAGE 111)

Passives with modals and modal-like expressions; passive infinitives

1 Passive with modals + *be* + past participle
   - Common modals: *can, could, might, may, should, must*
     Should the photos ***be taken*** in natural light?

2 Passive with modal-like expressions + (*to*) + *be* + past participle
   - Common expressions: *have to, need to, had better, be likely to, be supposed to*
     Rumors ***had better not be spread*** at this school.
     Good journalists ***don't need to be told*** what to do.

3 Passive infinitives (verb + *to be* + past participle)
   - Common verbs and expressions: *ask, be likely, expect, hope, refuse, seem*
     The problem ***isn't likely to be solved*** soon.

> **!** For negative sentences, use ***had better not + be*** + past participle.

A **Write sentences with passive forms.**

1 the facts / must / check / by the editor / _____ .
2 the manager / ask / show / the sales figures / _____ .
3 people / might / harm / by that false story / _____ .
4 the rumor / couldn't / control / _____ .
5 the journalists / refuse / tell / what to write / _____ .
6 that photo of me / had better / removed / from your post / _____ .

12.1 ADVERBS WITH ADJECTIVES AND ADVERBS (PAGE 119)

Adverbs with adjectives and adverbs

With adjectives

1 Use an adverb before an adjective to provide more detail about it.
   - Common adverbs: *especially, exceptionally, mainly, (not) necessarily, particularly, reasonably*
     John is ***especially skilled*** at painting, while his brother is ***mainly good*** at drawing.

2 Use an adverb before an adjective to say what the adjective is related to.
   - Common adverbs: *artistically, athletically, financially, musically, physically, scientifically, technically*
     Sandra is ***artistically talented*** in many ways, but she's not ***musically gifted*** at all.

With adverbs

3 Use an adverb before another adverb to provide more detail about it.
   - Common adverbs: *especially, exceptionally, particularly, reasonably*
     Some people are able to learn languages ***particularly easily***. For example, my friend Paolo learned five languages ***exceptionally fast***.

> **!** An adverb + an adjective describes a noun.
> _The concert_ was ***reasonably good***.
> An adverb + an adverb describes a verb.
> Sandra _paints_ ***exceptionally well*** for a beginner.

A **Circle the correct option.**

1 My accountant always gives me financially *correct / correctly* information.
2 Is she exceptionally *good / well* at music?
3 Jorge finished the test especially *quick / quickly*.
4 Eve learns new computer programs particularly *easy / easily*.
5 I like all kinds of music, but I'm mainly *interested / interestingly* in classical music.
6 Natasha's house is full of artistically *beautiful / beautifully* objects.

12.2 MAKING NON-COUNT NOUNS COUNTABLE (PAGE 121)

Making non-count nouns countable

Make non-count nouns countable with expressions describing specific quantities or amounts. For example:

1 Abstract ideas
   - a little bit of (kindness/luck/space/time)
     A little bit of kindness brightens up people's lives.
   - a piece of (advice/information)
     This is *a useful piece of information*.
   - a word of (advice/encouragement/sympathy/wisdom)
     He was full of *words of wisdom* and useful *pieces of advice*.

2 Activities and sports
   - a game of (basketball/chess/soccer/tennis)
     We played *a few games of basketball* over the weekend.

3 Food
   - a box of, a bunch of, a can of, a grain of, a loaf of, a package of, a piece/slice of, a pound of, a serving of
     I need *a bunch of parsley* and *a packet of cereal*.

   > **!** A pound = about .45 kilograms
   > A gallon = about 3.8 liters
   > A quart = about .95 liters

4 Liquids
   - a bottle of, a cup of, a glass of, a drop of, a gallon of, a quart of
     At the café, we ordered *two cups of coffee* and *a glass of juice*.

5 Miscellaneous
   - an act of (bravery/kindness)   Helping me move was *an act of kindness*.
   - an article/item of (clothing)   What is your favorite *item of clothing*?
   - a piece of (clothing/equipment/furniture/music/news)   That's a fantastic *piece of equipment*!
   - a work of (art)   This painting is my favorite *work of art*.

A **Complete the sentences with the words in the box. Use the plural form when necessary.**

act   article   game   serving   word   work

1 His _____ of encouragement really raised my spirits.
2 She gave each person a _____ of ice cream.
3 I think that being able to change yourself is a real _____ of bravery.
4 I lost three _____ of chess with my brother, and it ruined my evening.
5 I don't think we need any more _____ of art in this room.
6 How many _____ of clothing can you fit in that tiny suitcase?

VOCABULARY PRACTICE

7.1 POSITIVE EXPERIENCES (PAGE 67)

A Circle the correct options. Sometimes both are correct.

1 In my job, I have a positive effect on people. They *are of use / value* what I do.
2 I'm proud of the work I do. It *makes a contribution / is an honor* to work for this company.
3 My job is a lot of fun. I *take pleasure in / am a good influence on* my work.
4 It's good to make a contribution – to feel that what you do is *beneficial / worthwhile*.
5 When people are scared, it makes a difference if you *devote your life / reassure* them.
6 Janelle is an excellent nurse and *is a good influence on / devotes her life to* others.
7 When you do a job well, you generally *get satisfaction out of / reassure* it.
8 I want a job that has a positive effect on the world. I want to *make a contribution / make a difference*.

B Complete the sentences with these expressions. Sometimes more than one answer is correct.

devoted their lives to	get satisfaction out of	make a contribution	make a difference
reassure	take pleasure in	value	was beneficial
was of use	was worthwhile		

1 I enjoyed working on the construction of the new hospital. I felt it _____ for my city.
2 Thanks for your help. I always _____ the career advice you give me.
3 My sister and her husband have _____ helping others.
4 If we hire you, how can you help the company? How will you _____ ?
5 I often help people in trouble, and of course, I _____ that.
6 Don't worry. Let me _____ you everything will be fine.

7.2 MAKING PURCHASES (PAGE 68)

A Complete the conversation with the correct words.

be foolish	convinced me	look ridiculous	makes financial sense
practical	purchase	regret a purchase	

Marcy I think we should ¹_____ these snowboards.
Jason Yeah, the salesperson ²_____ it's cheaper than renting them.
Marcy It really ³_____ . We snowboard a lot in the winter, so it's ⁴_____ .
Jason But I'm not sure about these bright colors. I don't want to ⁵_____ in front of our friends.
Marcy I think they're really cool, but I don't want you to ⁶_____ that was kind of expensive. Why don't we go home and look at some other options online?
Jason Good idea. There's no reason to ⁷_____ and make a quick decision.

B Circle the correct option.

1 Owning an environmentally friendly car has a lot of *appeal / sense*, and I *convince / encourage* you to consider getting one.
2 For me, buying new clothes *is not worth the money / looks ridiculous*. I get bored with them after a couple of weeks, and I always *regret the purchase / urge you to buy them*.
3 My sister *regrets / urged me* to a buy a laptop, but I think this tablet *has potential / is foolish*, too. It's cheaper and will do everything I need it to.

8.1 DESCRIBING NEATNESS AND MESSINESS (PAGE 76)

A   **Circle the correct option. Sometimes both options are correct.**

1   We've *put the files in alphabetical order / folded the files* so they can be found easily.

2   Someone has *arranged the towels / hung up the towels* neatly.

3   He left his papers *all over the place / tangled up.*

4   She carefully *lined up / threw* the books on the shelves.

5   My dad *hung up his tools / put his tools in a pile* on the wall of his garage.

6   I keep telling my kids to *throw in / put away* their clothes.

7   All the dishes *are organized / are disorganized* neatly in the cupboard.

8   Your computer cables are all *jumbled up / tangled up.*

B   **Complete the paragraph with these expressions. Sometimes there's more than one correct answer.**

arranges	disorganized	fold	hangs up	jumbled up
leaves … all over the place		lines up	organized	puts away
tangled up	throws … on			

Leo and Ed are roommates, but they have completely different habits. Leo is ¹_____ . He always
²_____ his clothes neatly in the closet, and he ³_____
his shoes side by side on the floor. But Ed is completely ⁴_____ . His clothes are always
⁵_____ , and he ⁶_____ them _____ .
He doesn't ⁷_____ them, but just ⁸_____ them _____ the floor.

8.2 TALKING ABOUT PROGRESS (PAGE 78)

A   **Circle the correct option.**

1   My friend studied really hard, and *effectively / as expected*, she did well on her exams.

2   He does everything very quickly and *with ease / little by little.*

3   If you want to work on that project, you will have to do it *efficiently / on your own time*, not during work hours.

4   I researched the subject *thoroughly / smoothly*, but I still had trouble writing my essay.

5   It's a wonderful feeling to complete a project *successfully / steadily.*

6   I felt relaxed because I was allowed to work *with difficulty / at my own pace.*

B   **Put the words in parentheses ( ) in the correct place in each sentence. There's sometimes more than one correct place.**

1   I have to do this because it's easy to make mistakes. (little by little)

2   We read the instructions but couldn't find the information we wanted. (thoroughly)

3   Just work on it, and don't worry about the schedule. (steadily)

4   How can we manage this project? (effectively)

5   If you want to complete this, that's fine with me. (on your own time)

6   It's amazing that you can work in this noisy office. (efficiently)

7   I completed the project, and I didn't enjoy it at all. (with difficulty)

8   Everything went, so we were all very pleased. (smoothly)

9.1 LUCK AND CHOICE (PAGE 86)

A **Complete the sentences with the correct expressions.**

be in the right place at the right time
deliberate decision
fate
path

chance encounter
determination
believe my luck
was fortunate

1 A(n) _____ with a famous singer set me on a _____ to study music.

2 Sara believes in _____ . She says it's the reason she met her boyfriend, but I just think she happened to _____ .

3 Joaquin made a _____ to study law. He'll need a lot of _____ to finish his degree.

4 I _____ to get the last two concert tickets. I can't _____ !

B **Circle the correct options.**

1 College was a *life-changing experience / fate* for me.

2 Laura got a *path / lucky break* when she was asked to appear on a reality TV cooking show.

3 Seeing my cousin at the mall was a *right place at the right time / coincidence*.

4 Gavin studied biology, but he *wound up / was fortunate* being a gym teacher.

5 She made a *chance encounter / deliberate decision* to cancel her trip when she heard about the storm.

9.2 COMMENTING ON MISTAKES (PAGE 89)

A **Circle the correct options.**

1 Now I realize it was a bad *side / move*. It was a dumb *mistake / thing* to do.

2 My clothes were totally wrong for the party. I found myself in an *awkward / incompetent* situation, but I could see the *bad / funny* side of it.

3 I tripped over a bench because I wasn't *watching / learning* what I was doing. I don't text while walking now, but I learned that the *silly / hard* way.

4 Her dog bit me, which was *incompetent / unfortunate*. It *was my own fault / kicked myself* because I accidentally scared it.

5 It was a *hard / silly* mistake. And I made it because I was in too much of a *hurry / move*.

B **Complete the sentences with the expressions in the box.**

dumb thing to do   incompetent at   kicked myself   learned that the hard way
found myself in an awkward situation   sees the funny side   too much of a hurry   unfortunate

1 Because I was quite _____ math, I decided not to become an engineer.

2 I couldn't remember the company director's name, so I _____ .

3 I left my phone outside. Phones don't like rain! I _____ .

4 I tried to carry six glasses. It was a _____ .

5 Out of everyone in the restaurant, I was the one hit by the flying tomato! I was so _____ .

6 At the airport, I realized I'd forgotten my passport. I could have _____ !

7 Take your time. You're always in _____ .

8 He's a pretty positive guy. He usually _____ of things.

10.1 DESCRIBING CHARACTERISTICS (PAGE 98)

A **What are the sentences describing? Write the correct expression.**

a look	a match	build	features	look-alikes

1 Tom is very tall and has a lot of muscles. _____
2 Mike and Joey aren't related, but people think they're brothers. _____
3 I love the clothes my Aunt Larisa wears, and she always has a trendy hairstyle. _____
4 Mario has dark eyes, a small nose, and a wide mouth. _____
5 Jim and Cara are great for each other. They have a lot in common and get along well. _____

B **Circle the correct options.**

1 My brother and I have similar features and *likeness / characteristics*, but our interests are completely different.
2 You have to complete the form with your name, contact information, and *feature / gender*.
3 My dog Charlie is a *male / female*, and he's very shy.
4 The *features / similarities* between Isabel and her cousin make them seem more like sisters.
5 John is a very independent *individual / match*. He always does what he wants, even if it's not popular.
6 Lara has a medium *build / look*, while her sister is really tall and slim.

10.2 DESCRIBING RESEARCH (PAGE 100)

A **Circle the correct options.**

We did a ¹*survey / calculation* of our customers two months ago. One of the marketing staff then ²*analyzed / demonstrated* their profiles and ³*calculated / identified* ten customers who could become our special advisers. We want them to ⁴*examine / survey* our menu and give their ⁵*survey / assessment* of which dishes no longer interest people. In return for their help, we will give them cooking classes, including ⁶*demonstrations / analysis* and hands-on lessons. In addition, the manager has ⁷*examined / calculated* that we can afford to pay them $50 each for their time.

B **Complete the sentences with the correct words. Sometimes there's more than one correct answer.**

analyze	assessed	assessments	calculations
demonstrations	examined	identify	surveys

1 Would you please _____ this sales report and let me know if it's reliable?
2 I carefully _____ the printer, but I didn't see anything wrong with it.
3 We watched a couple of interesting _____ of how to interview new graduates.
4 I've _____ the information and am going to start writing my essay this afternoon.
5 We found out later that most of his _____ were wrong.
6 Unfortunately, the results of both customer _____ were unclear.
7 Can you _____ one or two employees who have the potential to be managers?

11.1 DESCRIBING CONSUMER GOODS (PAGE 108)

A Complete the sentences with the correct words in the box. Sometimes there is more than one correct answer.

> authentic   counterfeit   deadly   fake   fireproof
> genuine   inferior   legal   second-rate   sophisticated

1 Is this watch real or not? If it's a copy, it's a very _____ one.
2 Don't buy that phone. It's made of cheap, _____ materials, which won't last.
3 Your purse is _____. It's definitely made by our company.
4 Is it _____ to copy designer clothing if you openly say it's not real?
5 One of the chemicals used in this hair dye is dangerous. In fact, it's _____. Throw it away!
6 I got a(n) _____ $5 bill in my change yesterday. I took it to the bank, and they gave me a real one.
7 This blanket is made of _____ material and is very safe for your child's bed.

B Circle the correct options.

My friend says she doesn't mind if goods are ¹counterfeit / sophisticated as long as they're cheap. But it's an ²inferior / illegal trade, so that's why I prefer to buy ³fake / genuine goods. Besides, I don't like ⁴second-rate / original stuff.

I bought some ⁵fireproof / inferior gloves because I often have barbecues in the summer. But it turned out they weren't ⁶a deadly / an authentic product. The design was ⁷imperfect / original and had many problems. To me, this was a ⁸fake / legal issue because of the risk of injury, so I went to the police.

11.2 DEGREES OF TRUTH (PAGE 110)

A Complete the sentences with the expressions in the box. There is one you won't use.

> controversial   dishonest   inaccurate   misinformation
> suspicious   trustworthy   urban legend   white lie

1 I never believe what Joe tells me because he's _____.
2 I told Julie a _____ because I didn't want to hurt her feelings.
3 I don't believe the _____ about the clown statue that came to life.
4 Making clones of animals is a(n) _____ issue.
5 That news article is _____. Over 21 million people live in Mexico City, not 11 million.
6 I always post articles on social media from _____ sites because I want to inform people about the truth.
7 Donna's story is _____. I don't think she was in Los Angeles. I wonder where she really was!

B Cross out the word that doesn't work in each sentence.

1 Although the information is true, that article is biased / inaccurate / controversial because the author is friends with the person she interviewed.
2 Did you really think the story of a man owning a 200-pound cat was real? It was just a hoax / a white lie / a rumor.
3 Janice's story sounds suspicious / exaggerated / trustworthy. I don't think she really was lost for 15 hours!
4 That photo is accurate / misleading / false. Sharks can't live in lakes.
5 Misinformation / Urban legends / Rumors are entertaining as long as they don't harm anyone.

12.1 SKILL AND PERFORMANCE (PAGE 118)

A **Circle the correct options.**

My friend Tasha is ¹*talented / analytical* in many creative fields. She's very ²*trained / artistic*, even though she's never taken an art class. She paints, draws, and is an excellent photographer. I like her paintings the best because they're so ³*imaginative / determined*. She's also very ⁴*athletic / musical* and is ⁵*a skilled / an intellectual* piano player. Her father taught her how to play when she was three. Even though she's ⁶*technical / gifted* in these creative areas and finds math difficult, she wants to be an engineer. She's ⁷*determined / musical*, but I don't think it's a ⁸*logical / competent* choice.

B **Complete the sentences with the correct words.**

analytical	athletic	competent	intellectual	technical	trained

1 Josh isn't a(n) _____ life coach, but he gives very good life advice.
2 Sarah likes her science classes because she has a very _____ mind.
3 You have to be a(n) _____ person to be able to run a marathon.
4 I need help with some _____ problems on my computer.
5 My accountant is very _____, but I prefer to keep track of my budget myself.
6 _____ games that require skill and knowledge make you smarter while you play them.

12.2 DESCRIBING EMOTIONAL IMPACT (PAGE 120)

A **Circle the correct options. Sometimes both are correct.**

1 I'm so happy! You've really *brightened up my day / made my day*.
2 I didn't like that movie. It *was a real downer / took my mind off my problems*.
3 His wonderful speech *stressed me out / left a lasting impression on me*.
4 Thanks so much! Your party *raised my spirits / got me down*.
5 The doctor was great. She *put my mind at rest / ruined my day*.
6 Seeing the new art sculptures in the park *did me good / captured my imagination*.

B **Cover exercise A. Complete the sentences with the verbs in the correct form.**

be	brighten	capture	do	get	leave	raise	ruin	stress	take

1 He says his work is _____ him out right now.
2 You need something to _____ your mind off your problems.
3 The things he said _____ a lasting impression on me.
4 It will _____ you good to get out of the house for a while.
5 Failing my exam yesterday _____ a real downer.
6 You can _____ up people's lives with just a smile.
7 The speaker's ideas really _____ our imagination last night.
8 This cloudy, rainy weather is _____ me down.
9 Going out to dinner and a movie should _____ your spirits.
10 That bad news _____ my day yesterday.

PROGRESS CHECK

Can you do these things? Check (✓) what you can do. Then write your answers in your notebook.

UNIT 7

Now I can ...

☐ describe positive experiences.

☐ use gerunds and infinitives after adjectives, nouns, and pronouns.

☐ talk about purchases.

☐ use infinitives after verbs with and without objects.

☐ bargain for a purchase.

☐ write a for-and-against essay.

Prove it

Write three sentences about something you get satisfaction out of, something you take pleasure in doing, and something that you value.

Write three sentences about how you spend your free time, how you waste time, and how people often spend weekends in your town.

Write two sentences about a practical purchase you've made and two sentences about a foolish purchase.

Complete the sentence with your own ideas.
Last year, I persuaded _____ .

Write down two expressions each for (1) bargaining, (2) accepting an offer, (3) rejecting an offer.

Look at your essay from lesson 7.4. Find three ways to make it better.

UNIT 8

Now I can ...

☐ describe neatness and messiness.

☐ use modal expressions with *be*.

☐ talk about progress.

☐ use future forms.

☐ suggest and show interest in ideas.

☐ write a complaint letter.

Prove it

Write four sentences using each of these expressions: *put sth in alphabetical order, arrange sth neatly, be jumbled up, put away.*

Complete the sentences.
We're supposed to _____ .
Don't worry. He's bound to _____ .

Complete the sentences.
These days, _____ is going smoothly.
I _____ with difficulty.

Write two predictions and two plans about your future.

Write your response to a suggestion to have a pool party this weekend. Then write another suggestion.

Look at your complaint letter from lesson 8.4. Find three ways to make it better.

UNIT 9

Now I can ...

☐ talk about luck and choice.

☐ use unreal conditionals.

☐ comment on mistakes.

☐ express wishes and regrets.

☐ reassure someone about a problem.

☐ write an article with tips.

Prove it

Complete the sentences: *I don't believe in _____ .*
Good things happened to me because of _____ .

Complete the sentence: *If I could _____ , I _____ .*

Complete the sentences to match the comment.
Recently, I _____ . That was a bad move.
Yesterday, I _____ . I wasn't watching what I was doing.
Once, I _____ , but luckily, I saw the funny side of it.

Complete the sentences about small things you regret.
I wish I could _____ .   If only I _____ .
I wish I hadn't _____ .

Complete these expressions of reassurance.
It's no use _____ .   What are you _____ ?

Look at your article from lesson 9.4. Find three ways to make it better.

PROGRESS CHECK

Can you do these things? Check (✓) what you can do. Then write your answers in your notebook.

Now I can …	Prove it
☐ describe people's characteristics.	Write three sentences about the features, build, and look of a well-known person.
☐ use gerunds after prepositions.	Complete the sentence: *I believe in* _____ .
☐ describe research.	Describe some analysis you would like to do on the grocery shopping habits of your class. How would you go about the research and what would the research demonstrate?
☐ use complements of verbs describing cause and effect.	Write four sentences. Use each of these verbs once: *enable, keep from, let, protect from.*
☐ give my impressions.	Complete the sentences about what your friends are doing or thinking about. *I have a hunch that* _____ . *I get the impression that* _____ .
☐ write a professional profile.	Look at your professional profile from lesson 10.4. Find three ways to make it better.

Now I can …	Prove it
☐ describe consumer goods.	Write sentences with these words: *authentic, fireproof, illegal, second-rate.*
☐ use passive forms.	Complete the sentences with passive forms and your own ideas. *This fake watch was* _____ . *One day, goods will* _____ *by* _____ .
☐ talk about degrees of truth.	Write sentences with these words: *accurate, dishonest, exaggerated, hoax.*
☐ use passives with modals and modal-like expressions; use passive infinitives.	Complete the sentence: *Fake purses shouldn't* _____ *online.*
☐ express belief and disbelief.	Write two expressions each for expressing belief, some belief, and disbelief.
☐ write a persuasive essay.	Look at your persuasive essay from lesson 11.4. Find three ways to make it better.

Now I can …	Prove it
☐ talk about skill and performance.	Write three sentences. Use a pair of words in each sentence: *analytical/logical, athletic/trained, musical/artistic.*
☐ use adverbs with adjectives and adverbs.	Complete the sentences with an adjective or adverb and your own ideas. *I sing especially* _____ . *Soccer is an athletically* _____ *sport.*
☐ describe emotional impact.	Write four sentences. Use each of these expressions once: *get me down, leave a lasting impression on me, make my day, stress me out.*
☐ make non-count nouns countable.	Complete the sentences. *My teacher gave me two* _____ *advice.* *How many* _____ *clothing are you taking?* *Are you free for a(n)* _____ *basketball?* *Everyone needs a(n)* _____ *kindness.*
☐ describe my ambitions.	Complete the sentences with your own ideas. *I'm determined to* _____ . *I'm confident that* _____ . *But I can't say for sure that* _____ .
☐ write a review of a performance.	Look at your review from lesson 12.4. Find three ways to make it better.

This page is intentionally left blank

PAIR WORK PRACTICE (STUDENT A)

7.3 EXERCISE 5 STUDENT A

Conversation 1

Read the information. Then use these arguments while bargaining to get the best price from Student B.

Situation: You want to sell your mountain bike for $175 (your opening price can be higher).

- It's very strong and reliable.
- You've only used it for a few months. It has no damage.
- It's a popular model. Mountain bikers love it.
- You can throw in a lock for free.

Conversation 2

Situation: You want to buy a couch from Student B. Find out the price and bargain hard to get the best deal.

9.3 EXERCISE 3C STUDENT A

Conversation 1

You and Student B are close friends.

Problem: You forgot your eight-year-old nephew's birthday, and he's really upset. Tell your friend about it and ask for advice.

Conversation 2

You are a professor. Student B is your student. Listen to Student B's problem and give advice. Reassure them, using expressions that are appropriate for your relationship.

10.3 EXERCISE 5A

Discuss the gyms, giving your impressions of each. Decide which one you'd each like to join, and why.

	Gym 1	Gym 2	Gym 3
Cost	Programs for all budgets	Student discounts	Pay by month or by year
Location	Two locations: uptown and downtown	Six convenient central locations	One convenient central location
Classes	50 classes a week: yoga, dance, swimming, diet and weight loss	Boxing, karate, judo, personal training	Fitness classes, 8 large studios, personal trainers, athletic training
Equipment	Weights, running machines	Weights, running, and cycling machines	modern equipment, wall/rope climbing
Social area	Wi-Fi, healthy snack bar	TVs, Wi-Fi, café and juice bar	Café, lounge, TVs, Wi-Fi
Pool	Large changing rooms	✗	Clean changing room, spa
Hours	Open daily 8:00 a.m. to 10:00 p.m.	Open 24/7	Open 6:00 a.m. to midnight

PAIR WORK PRACTICE (STUDENT B)

7.3 EXERCISE 5 STUDENT B

Conversation 1

Situation: You want to buy a mountain bike from Student A. Find out the price and bargain hard to get the best deal for yourself.

Conversation 2

Read the information. Then use these arguments while bargaining to get the best price from Student A.

Situation: You want to sell your large couch for $200 (your opening price can be higher).

- It's in excellent condition, almost new.
- It's large and seats three people comfortably.
- It's a very stylish dark-gray color. The material is very strong.
- You can throw in three pillows for free.

9.3 EXERCISE 3C STUDENT B

Conversation 1

You and Student A are close friends.

Listen to Student A's problem and give advice. Reassure them, using expressions that are appropriate for your relationship.

Conversation 2

You are a student. Student A is your professor.

Problem: You have failed two tests recently. You are worried about the future of your studies. Tell your professor about it and ask for advice.

This page is intentionally left blank